The Cat Lovers Coloring Book

50 Grayscale Cats to Color

Perfect for relaxation and fun!

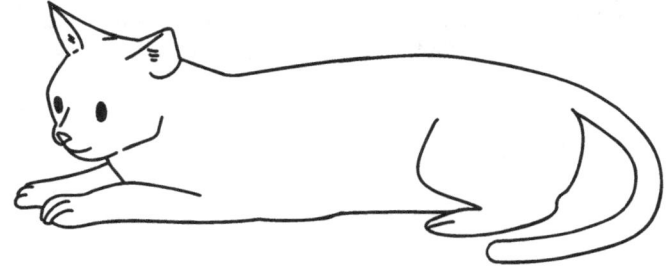

If you're anything like me, the first time you saw a grayscale coloring book you were like, "Whaaat?"

You may have even thought that when you saw this coloring book, but as you will soon discover, coloring with grayscale as your guide produces much more in-depth and interesting pictures in less time than many traditional black and white coloring between the lines variety of coloring books because you're focusing on coloring not shading. Think of it a bit like a paint by numbers, but without the numbers and with the shading already done for you. The shades of gray in grayscale coloring will tell you where you should apply light or dark colors in the picture. Generally speaking, light colors will go over light gray, dark colors will go over dark gray and medium colors can be used on either. But, of course, this is about creativity and fun, so you need to focus on what you want to do, how you want the picture to turn out and most of all what makes you feel the best about your coloring experience.

If you want to find out more about coloring in grayscale, there's a lot of great information out there. Just do a basic search and you'll find out just what you want to know.

Have fun!

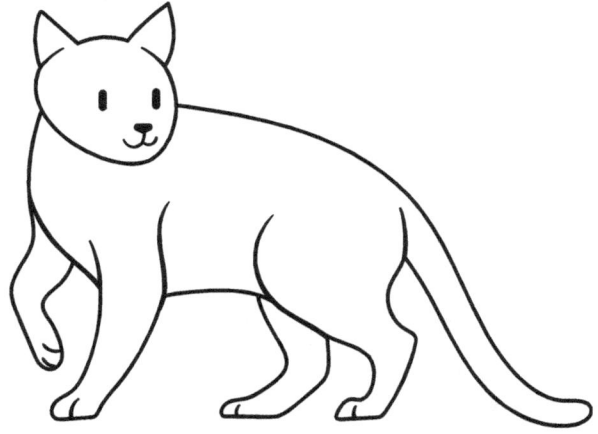

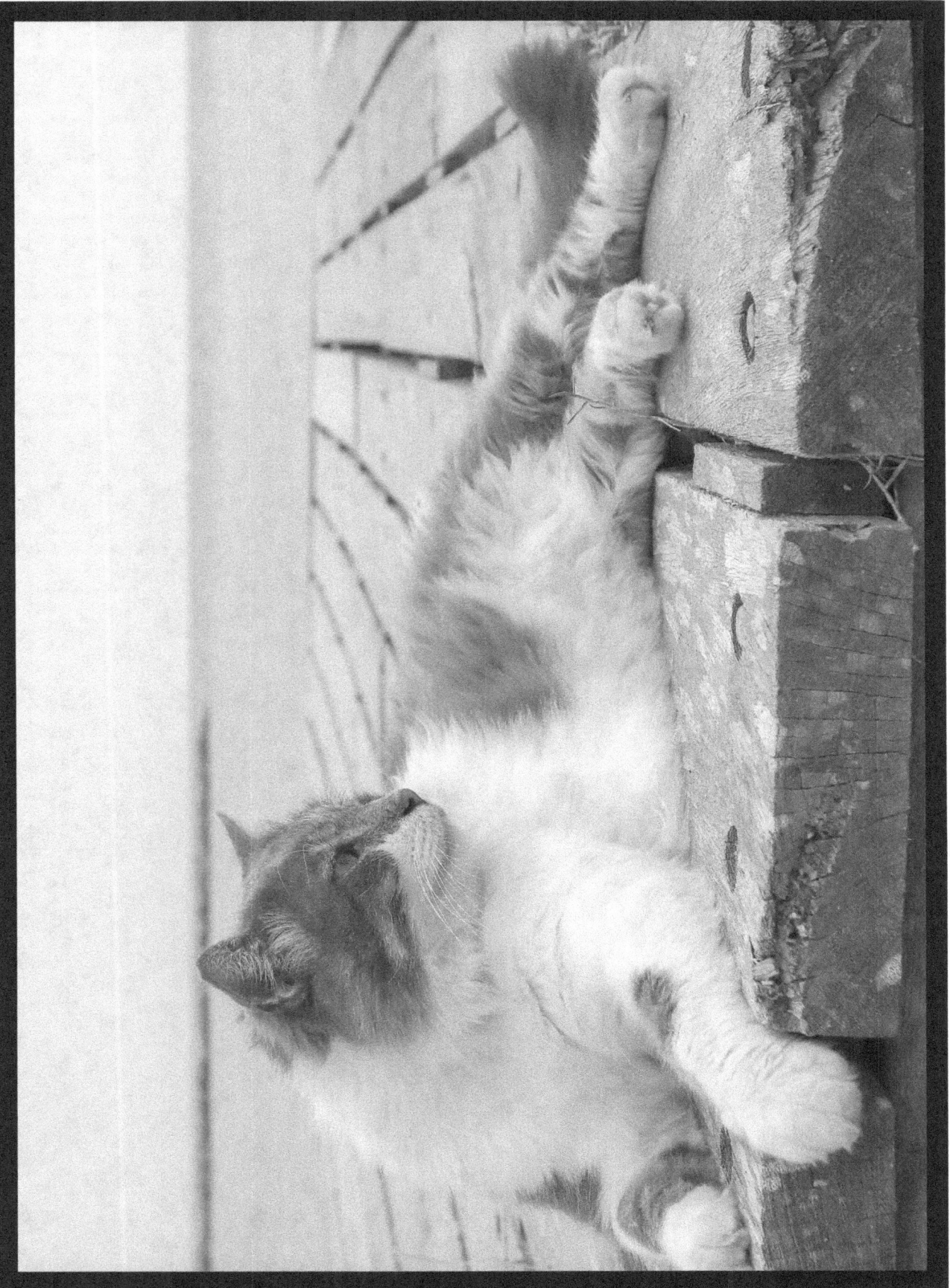

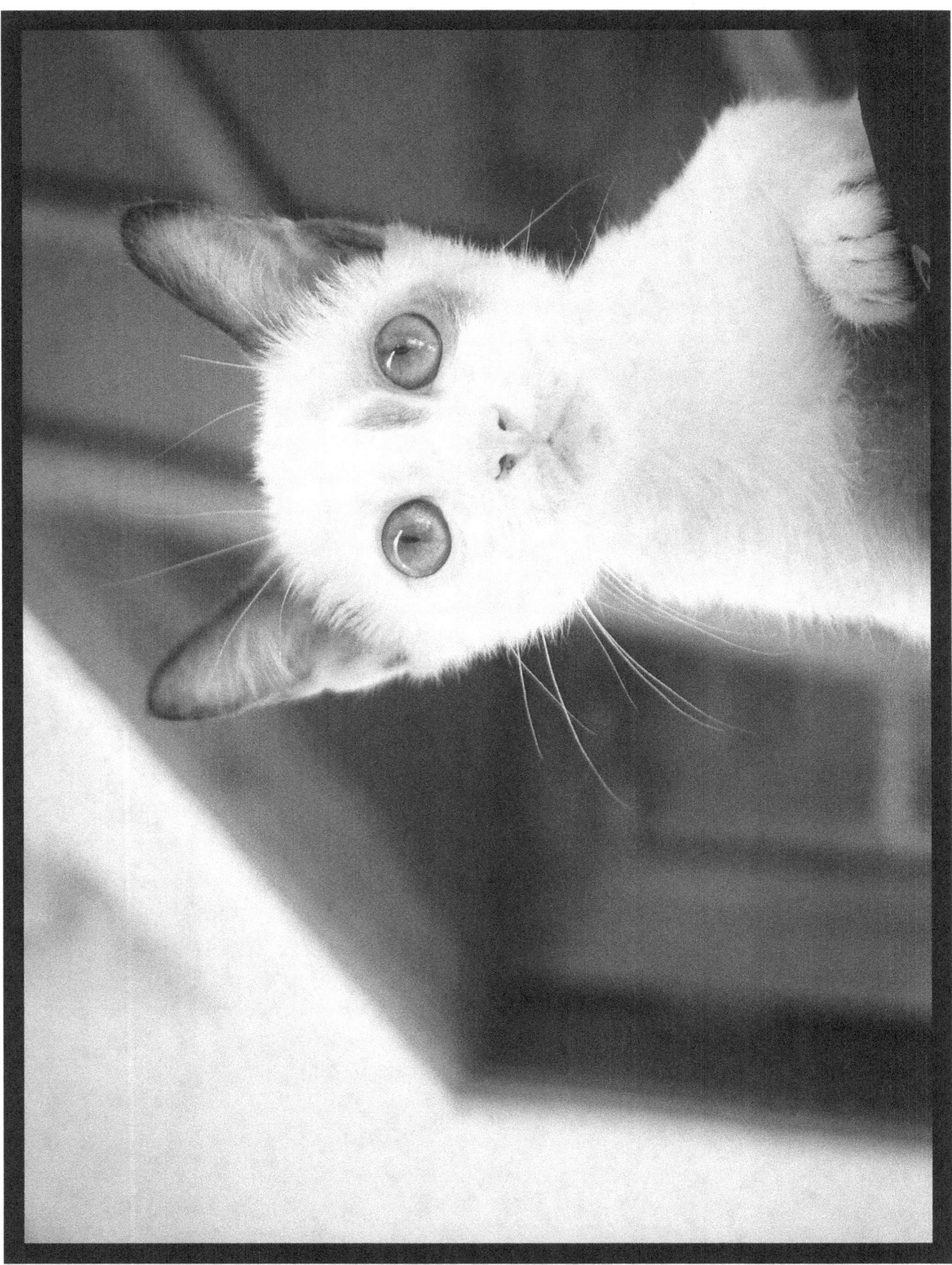

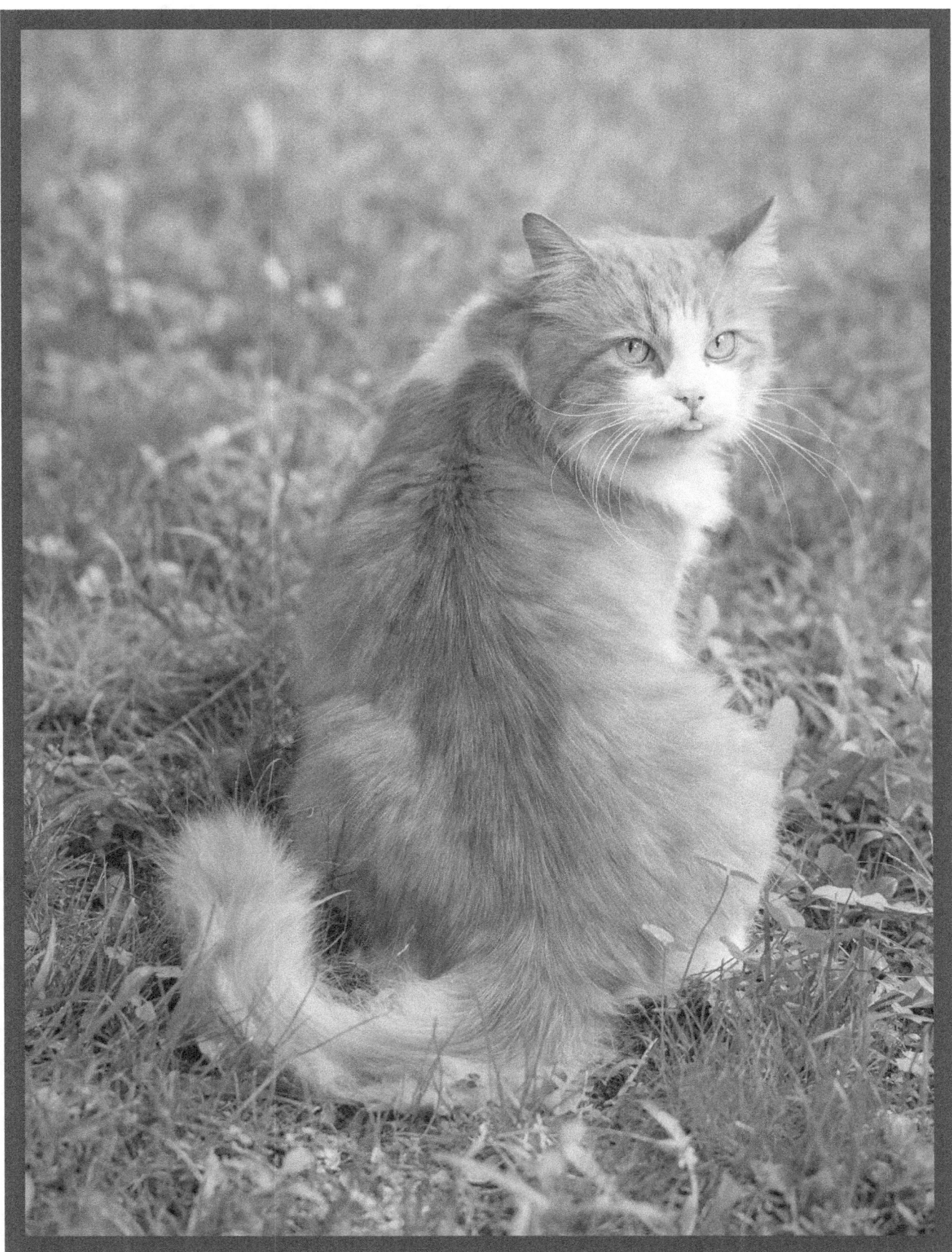

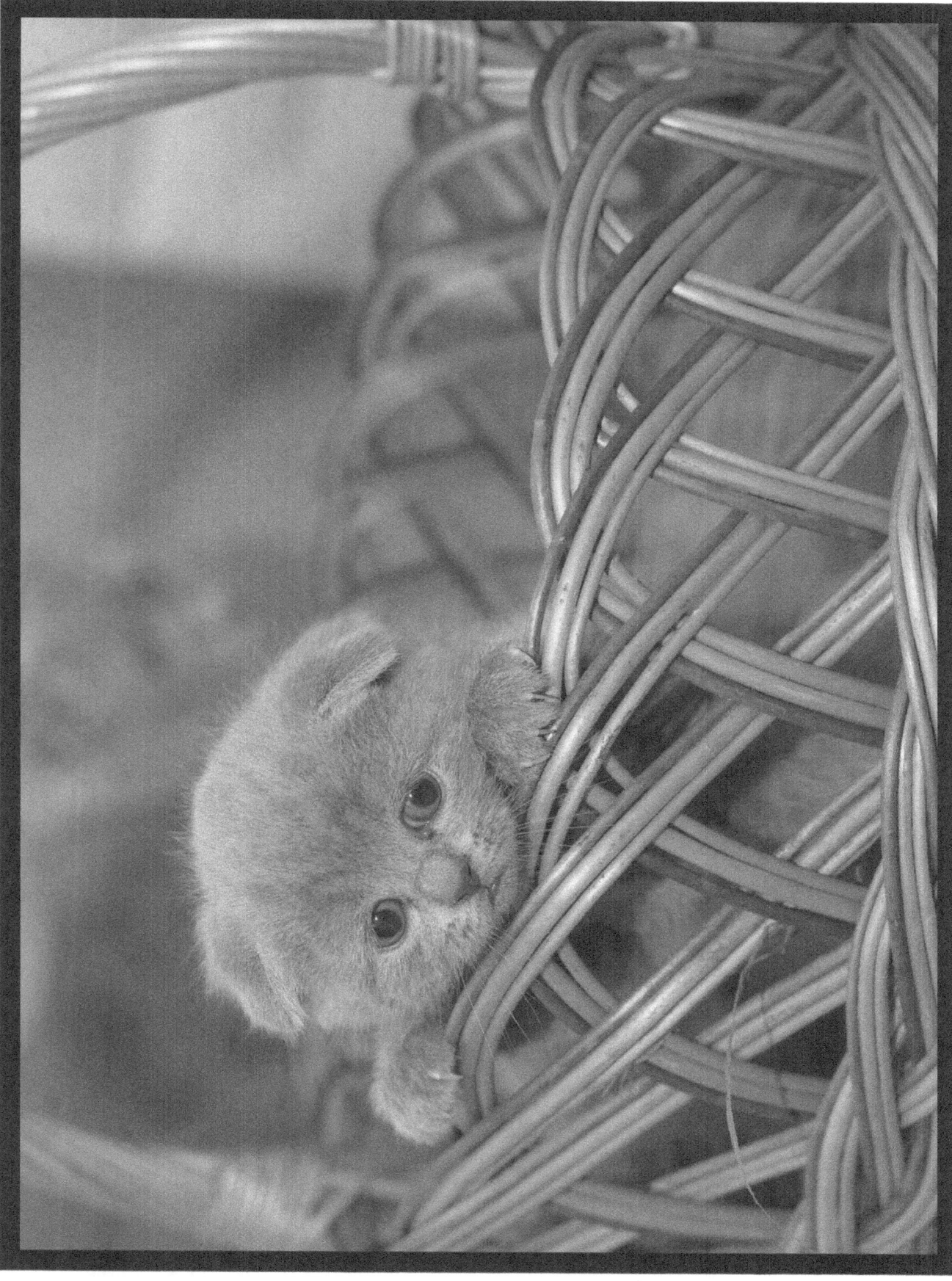

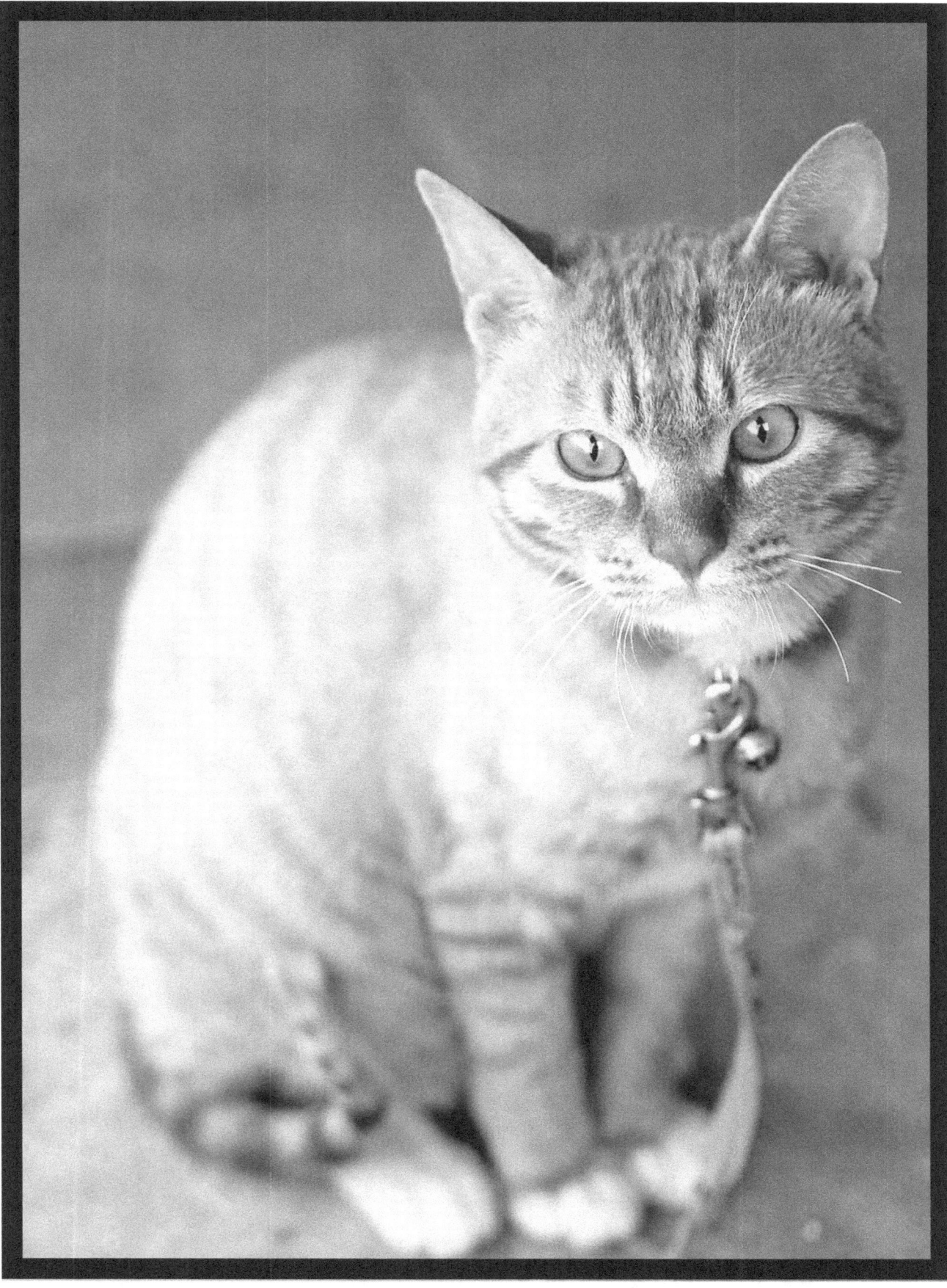

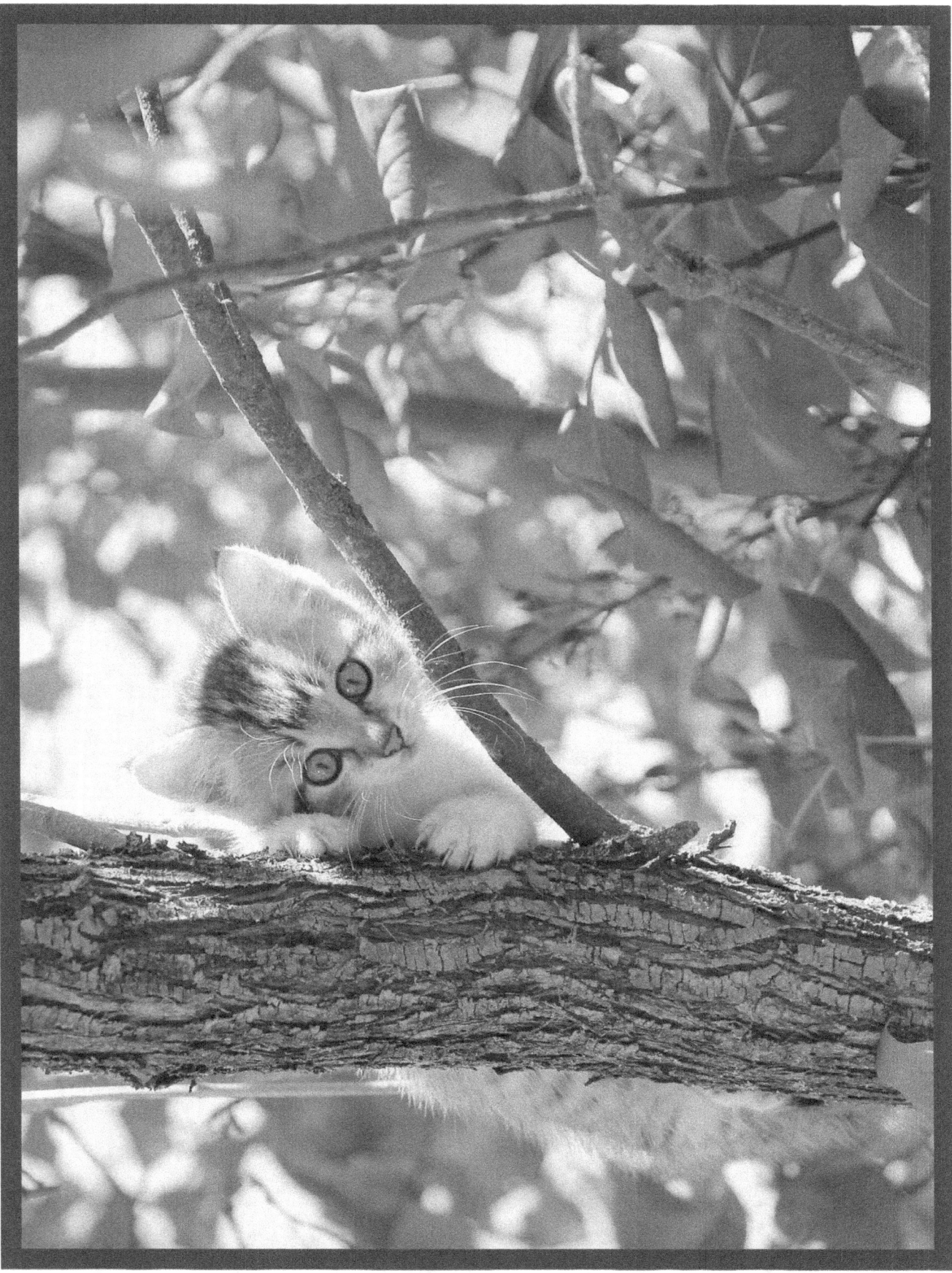

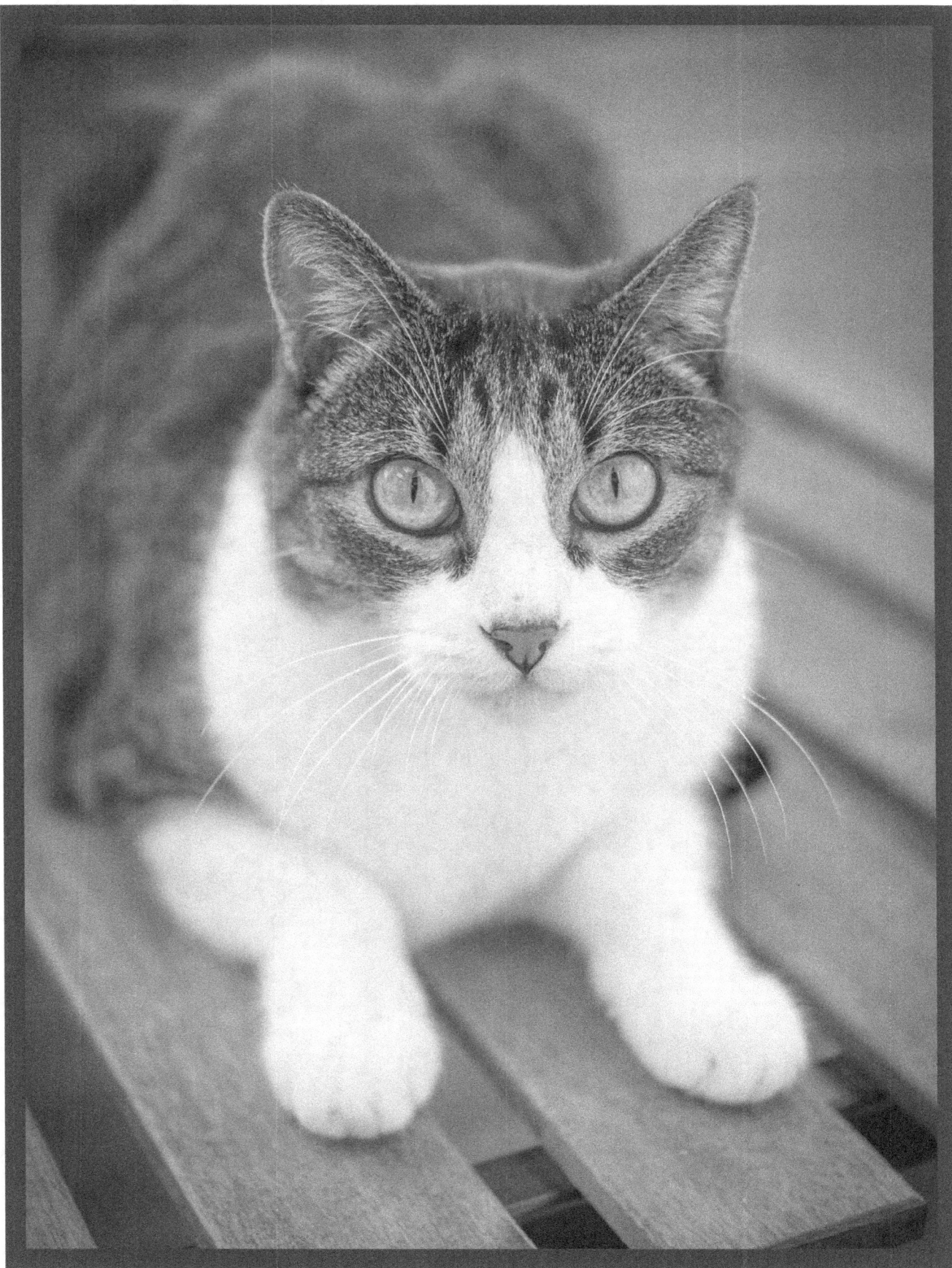

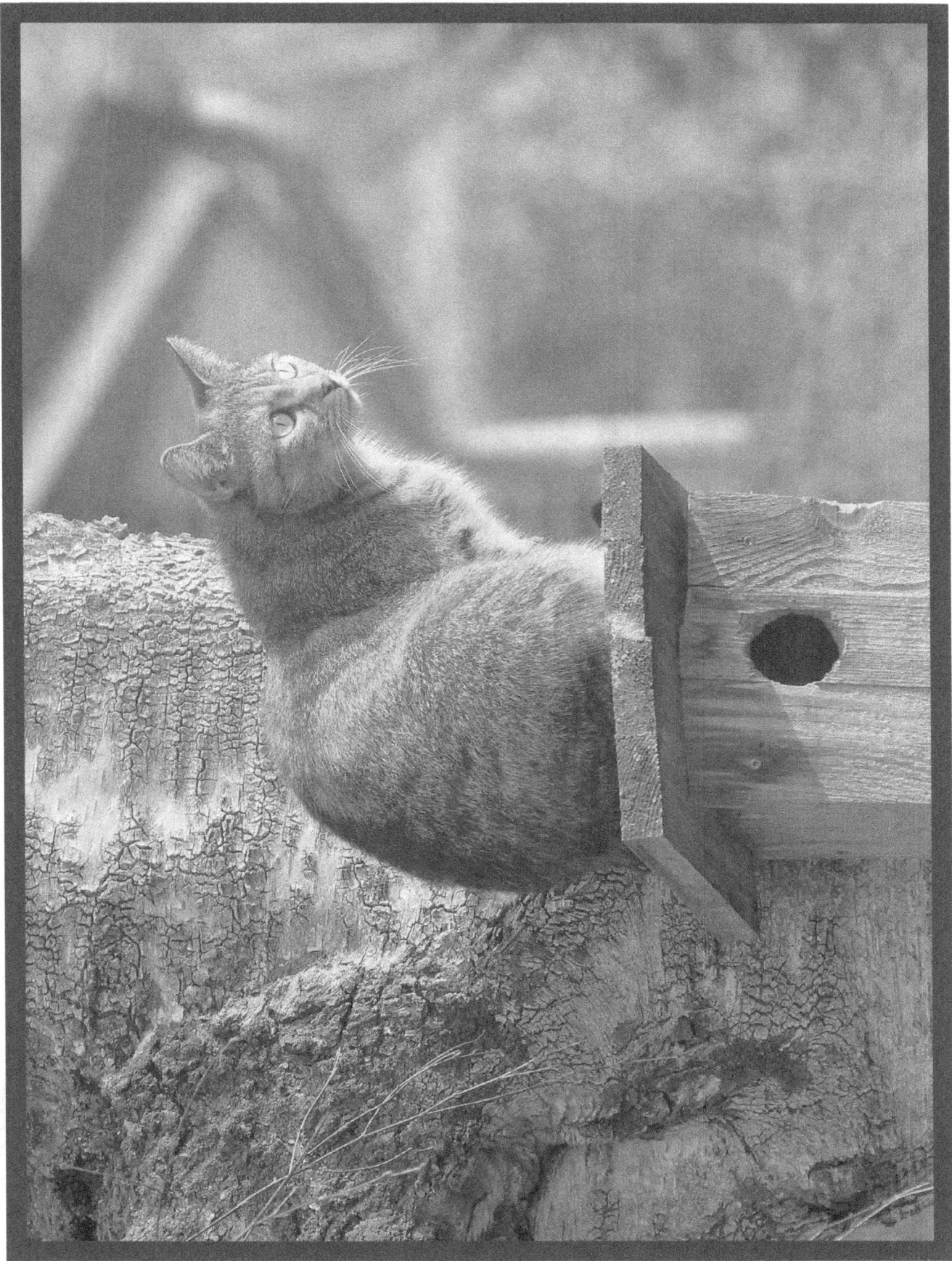

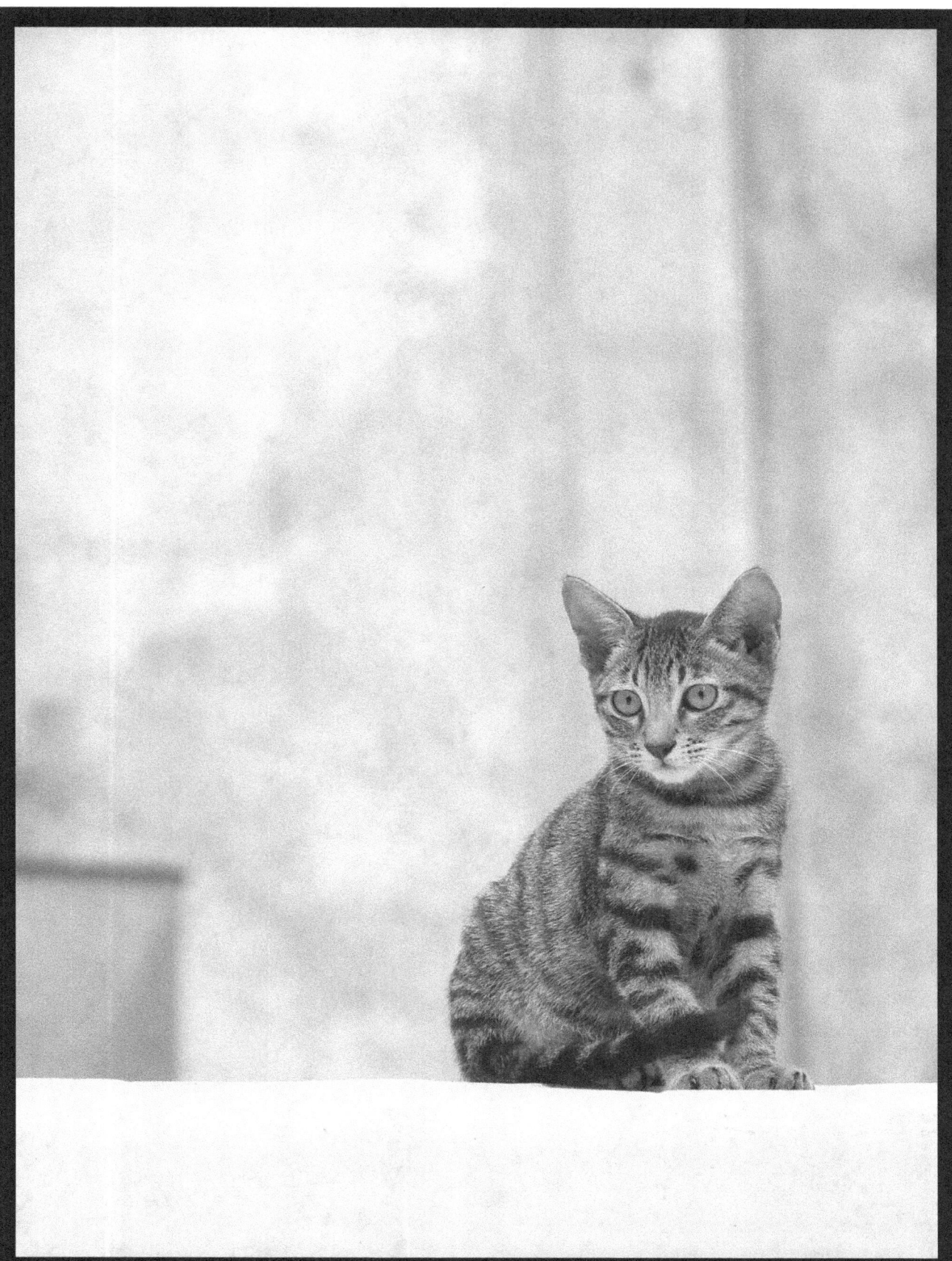

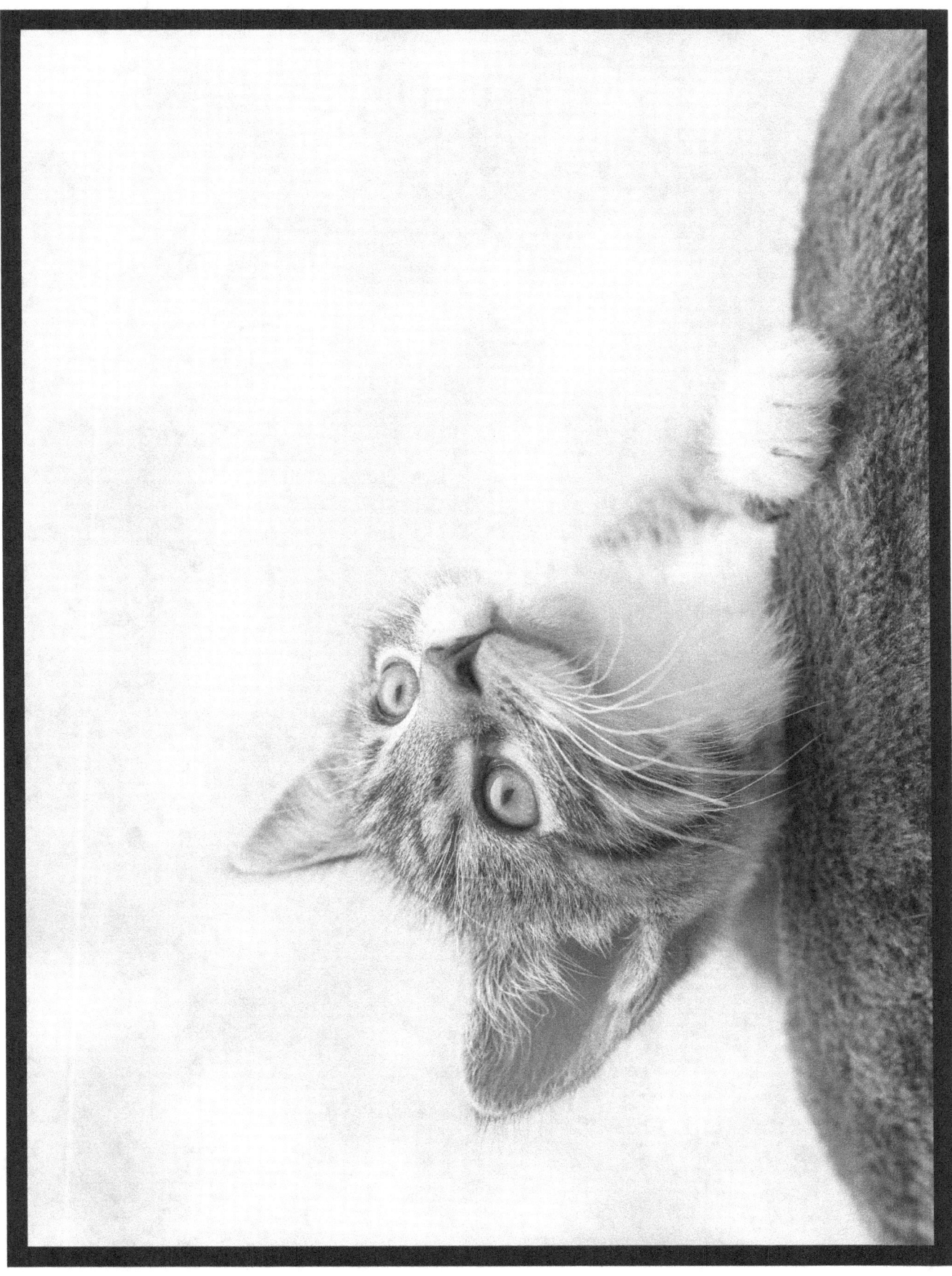

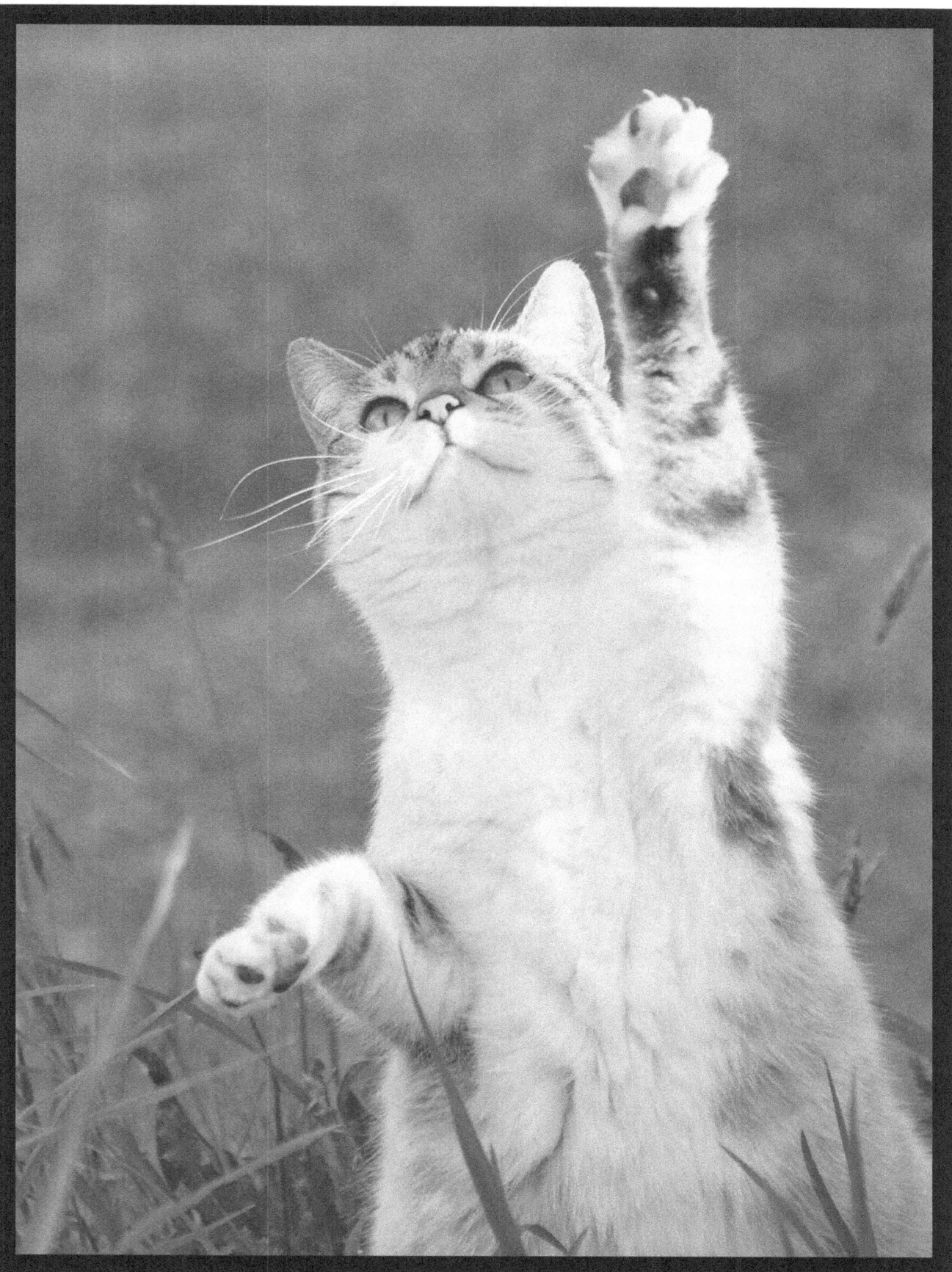

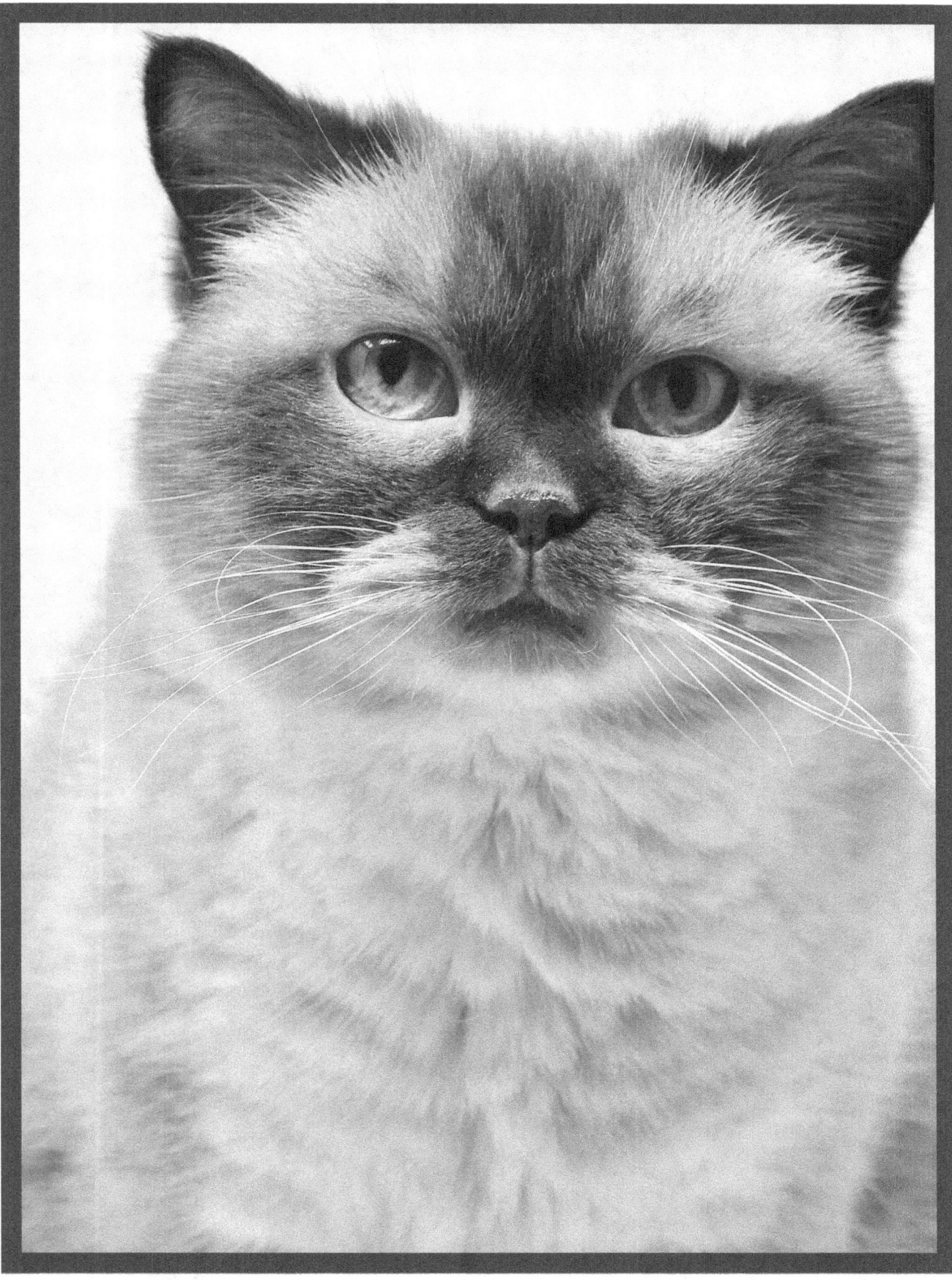

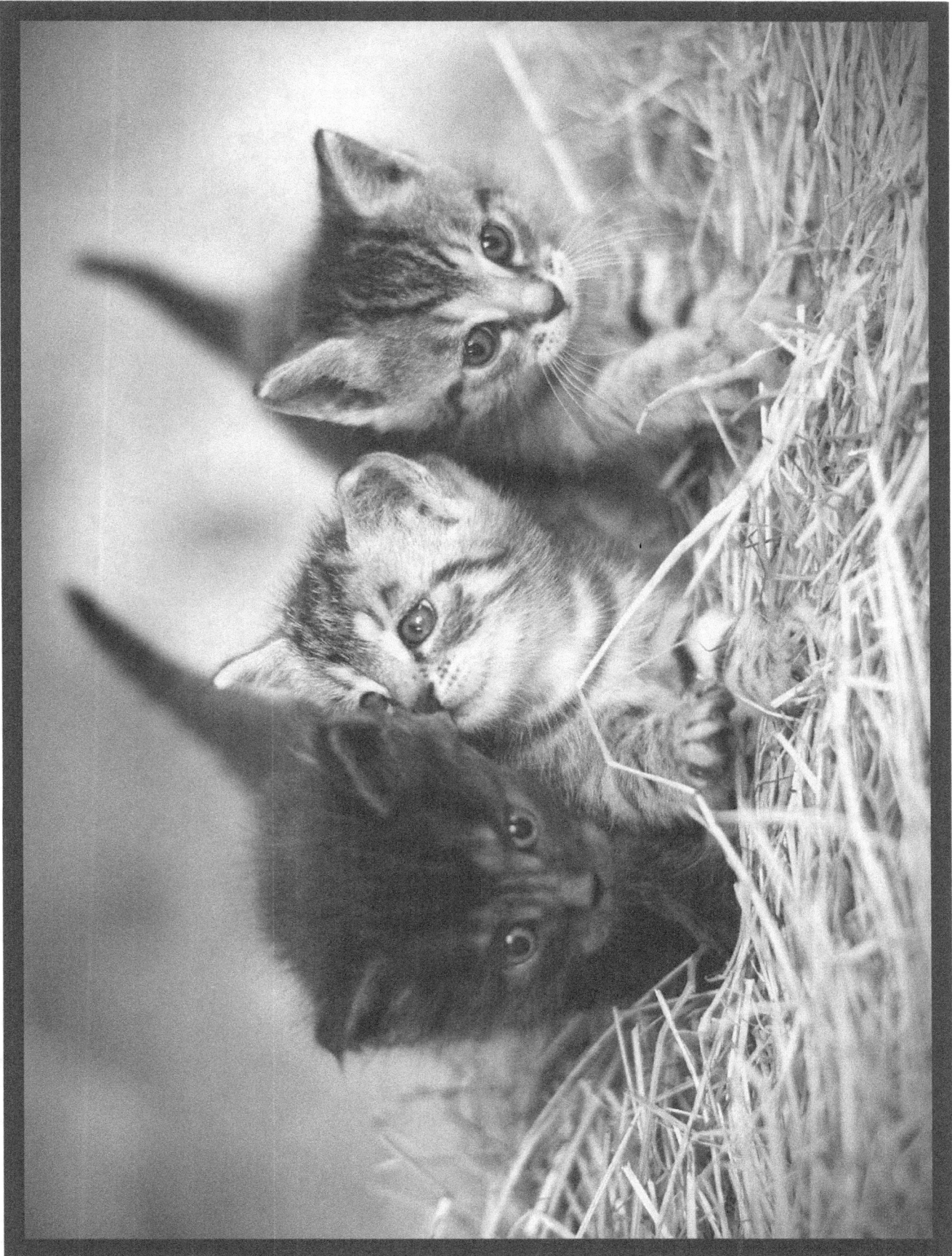

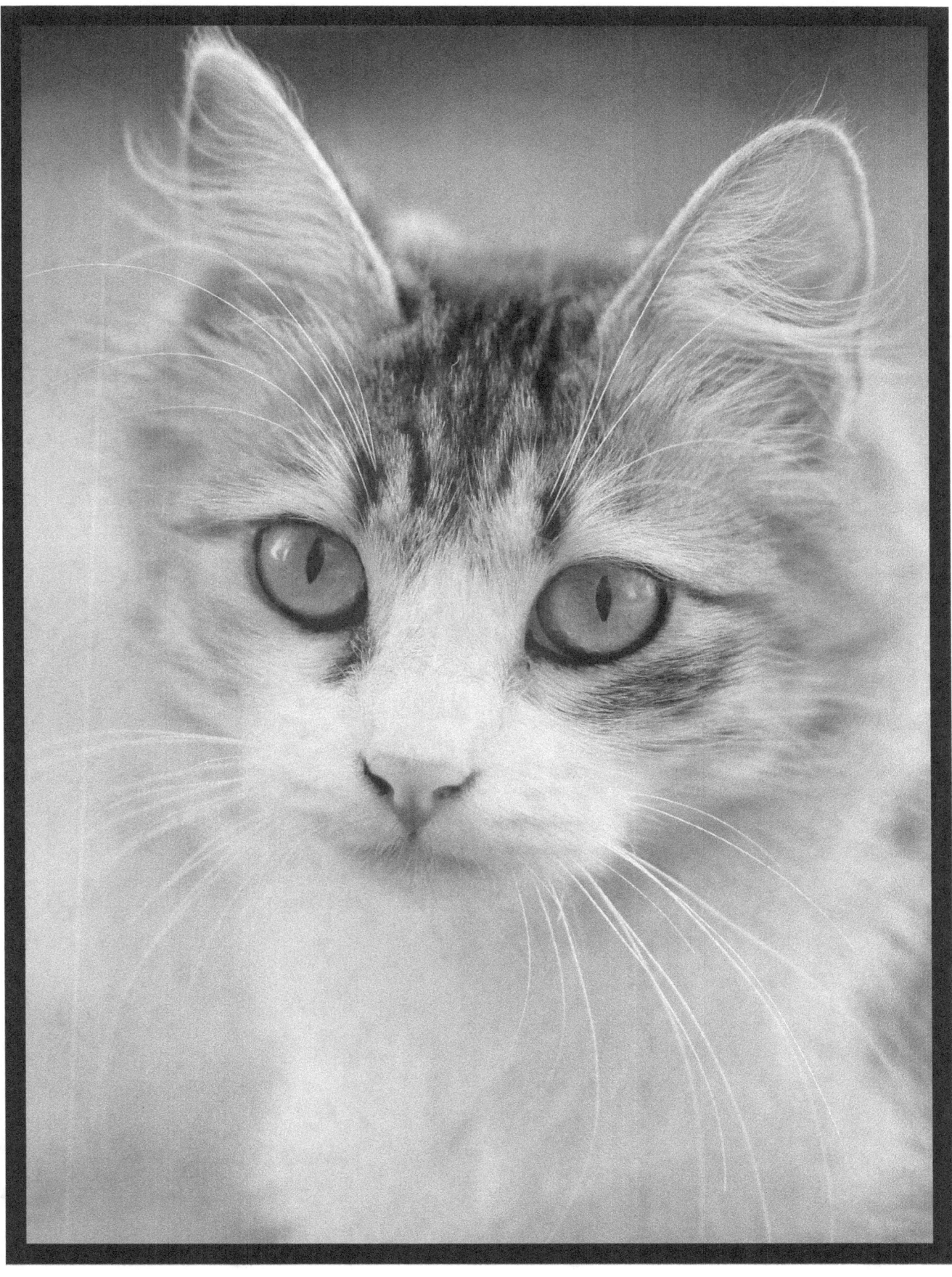

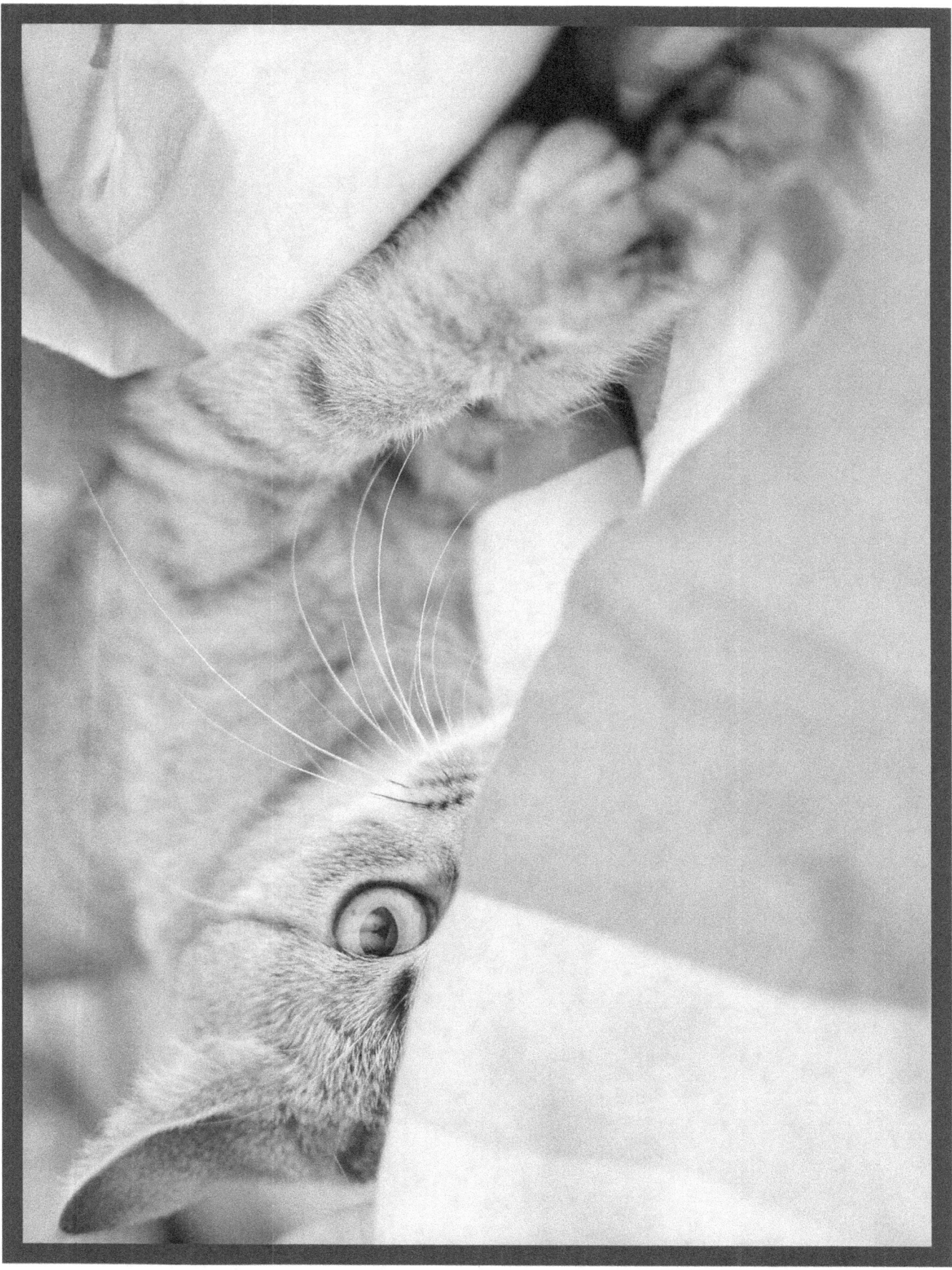

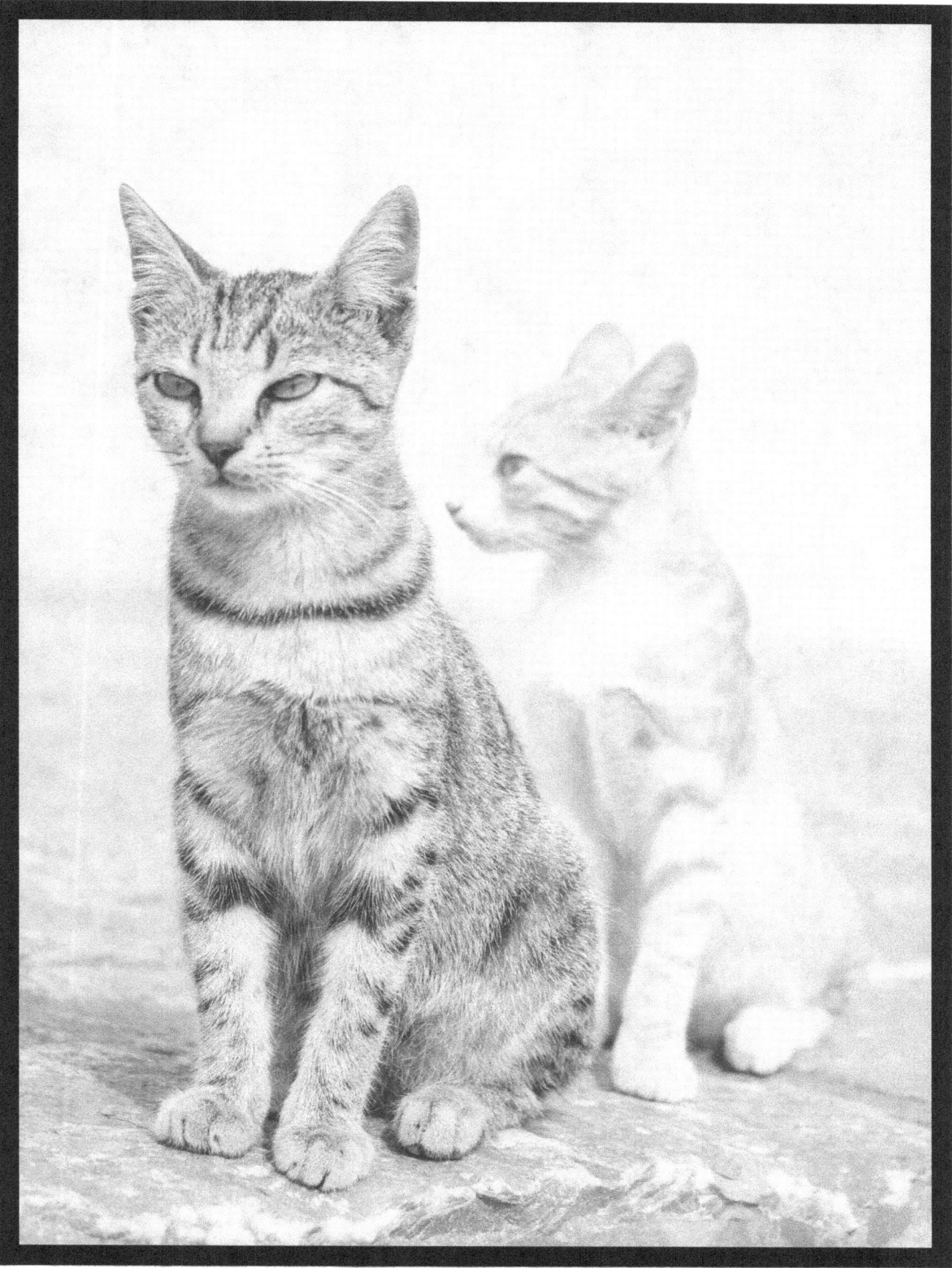

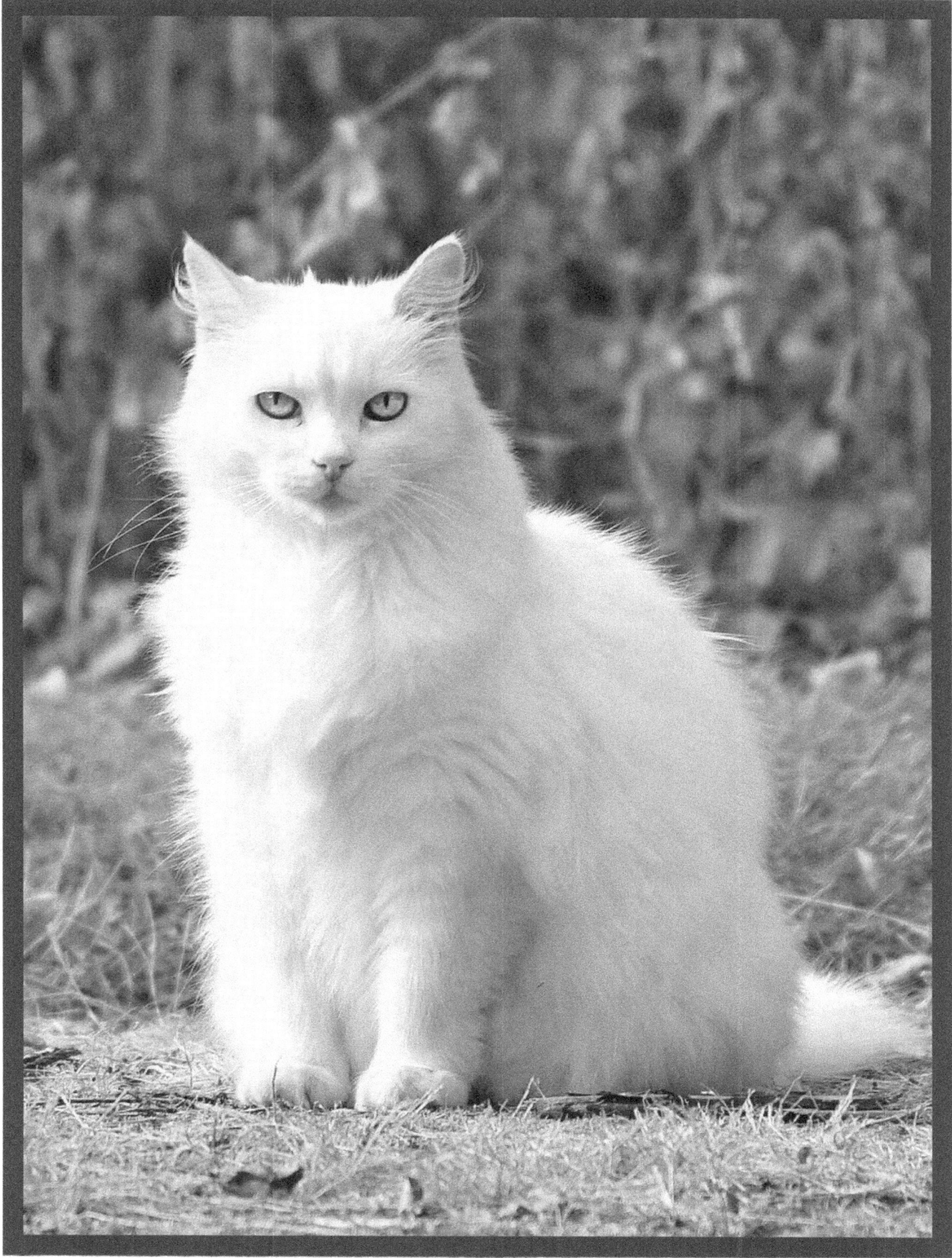

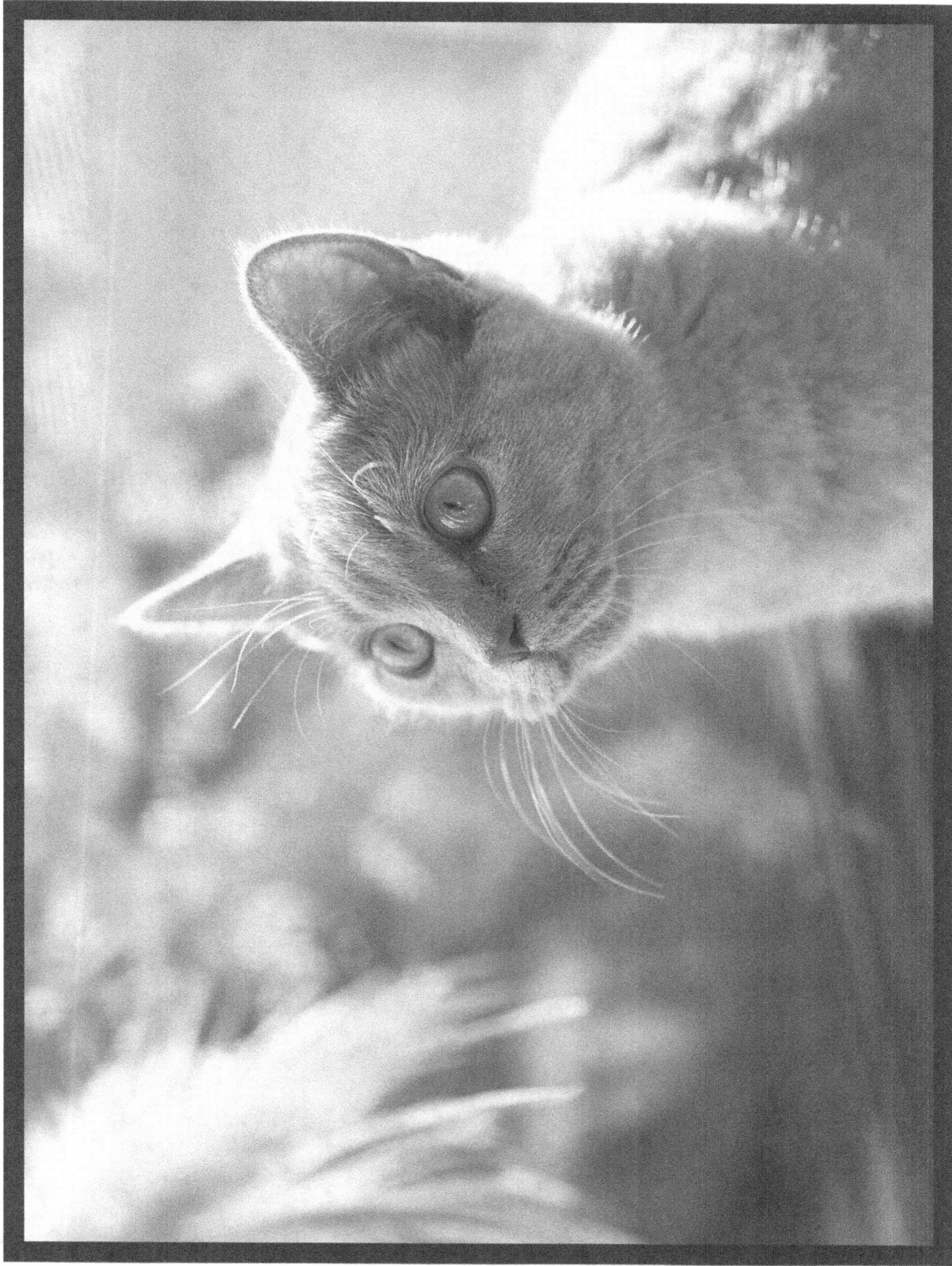

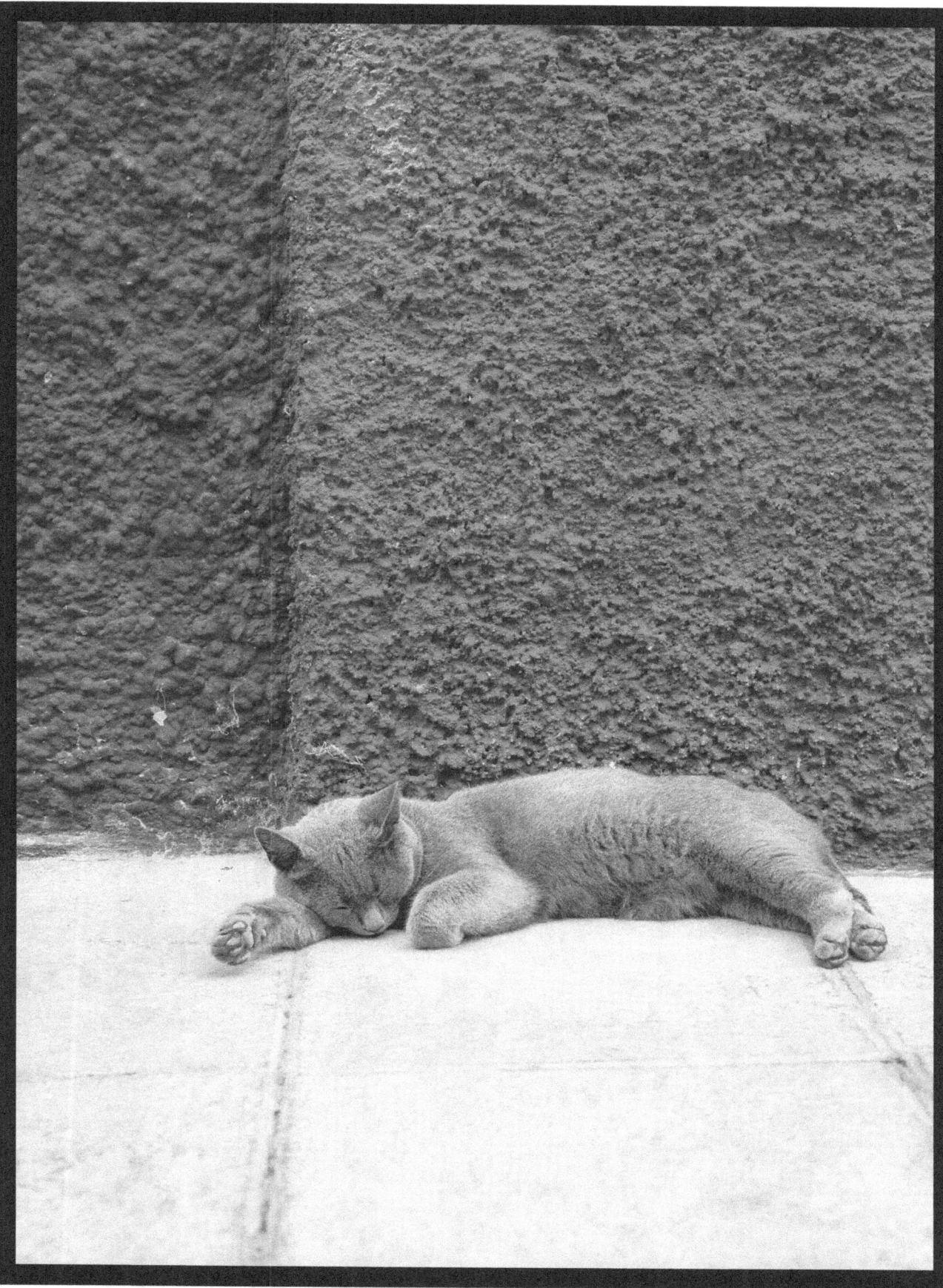

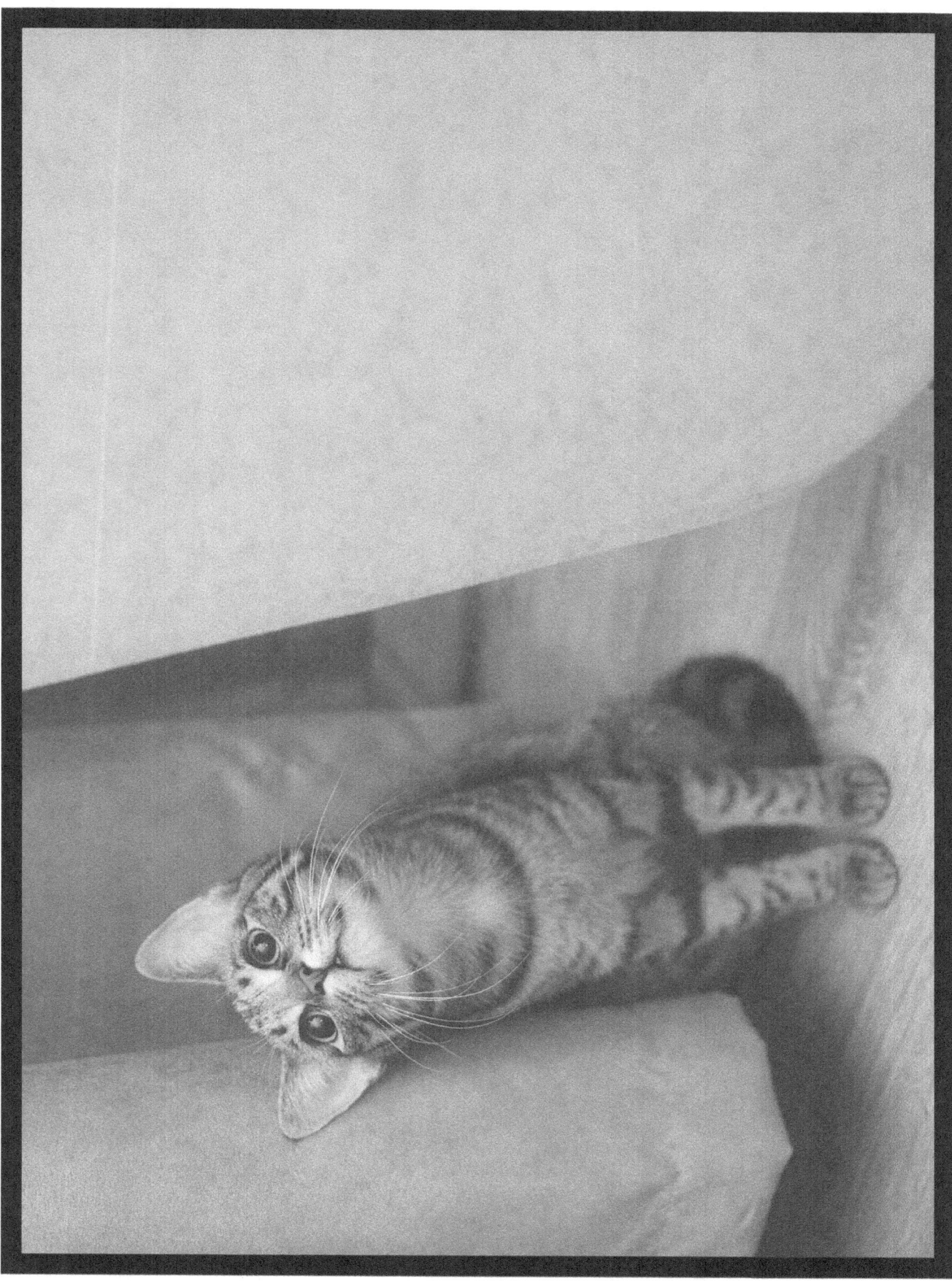

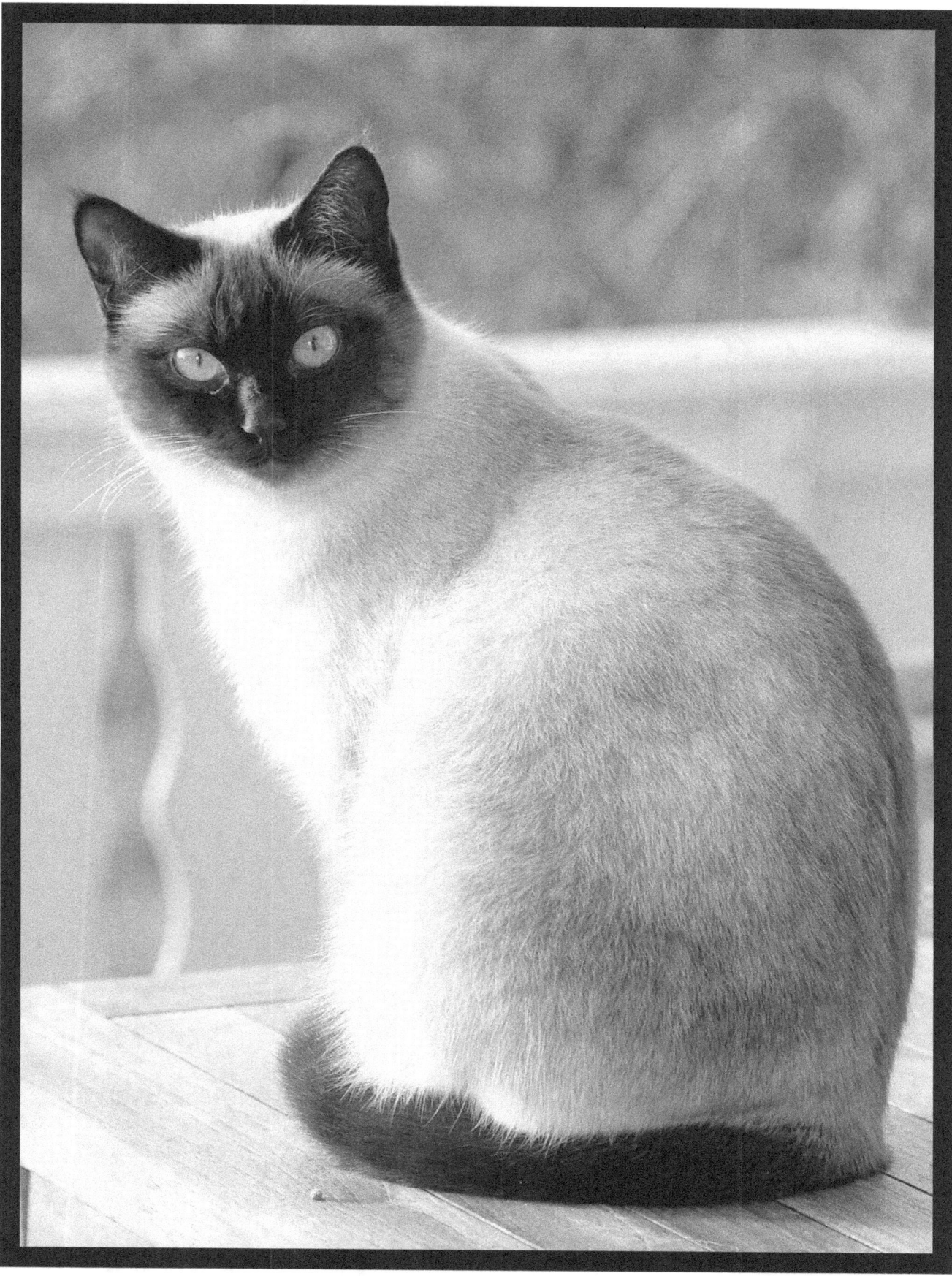

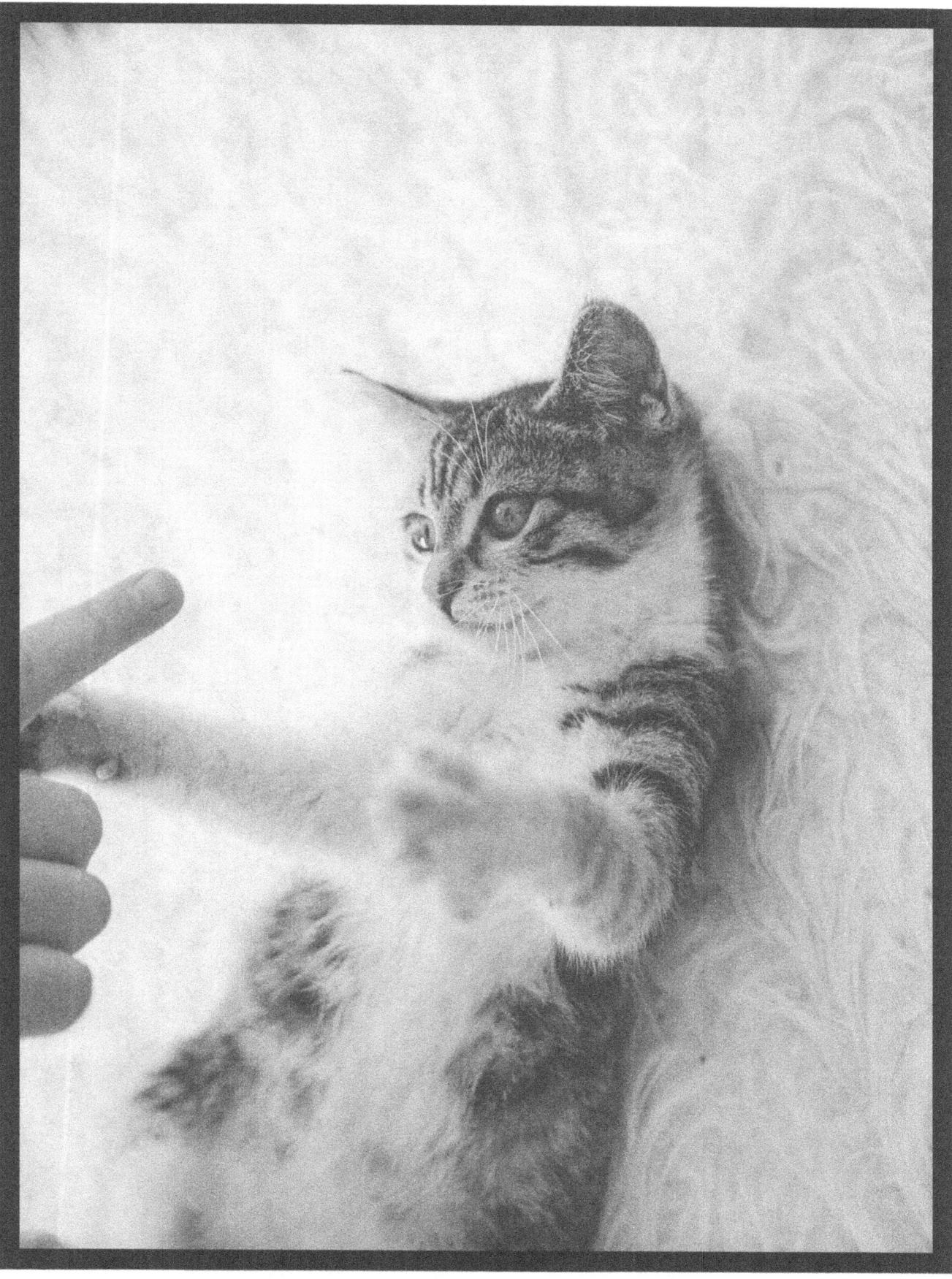

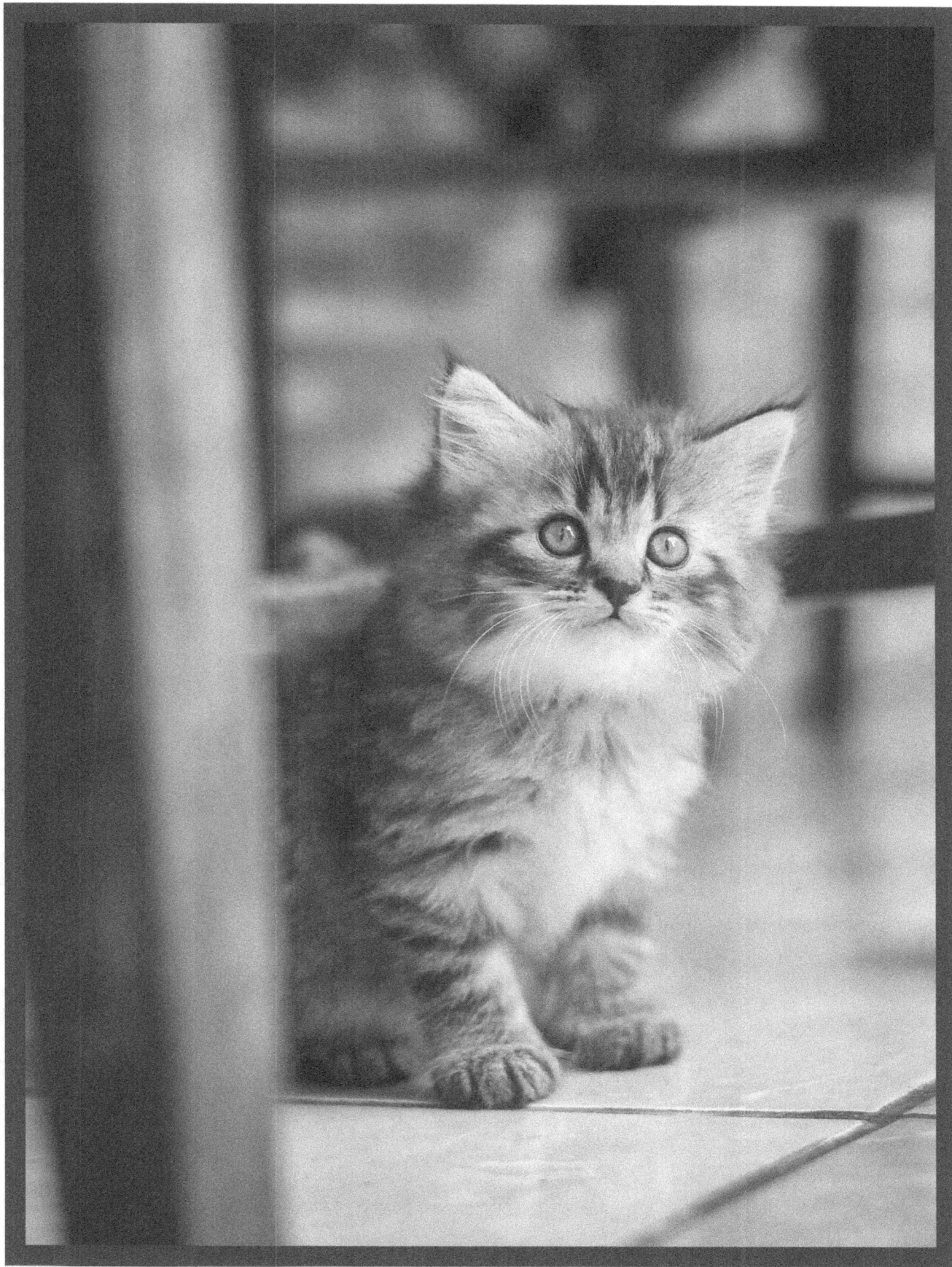

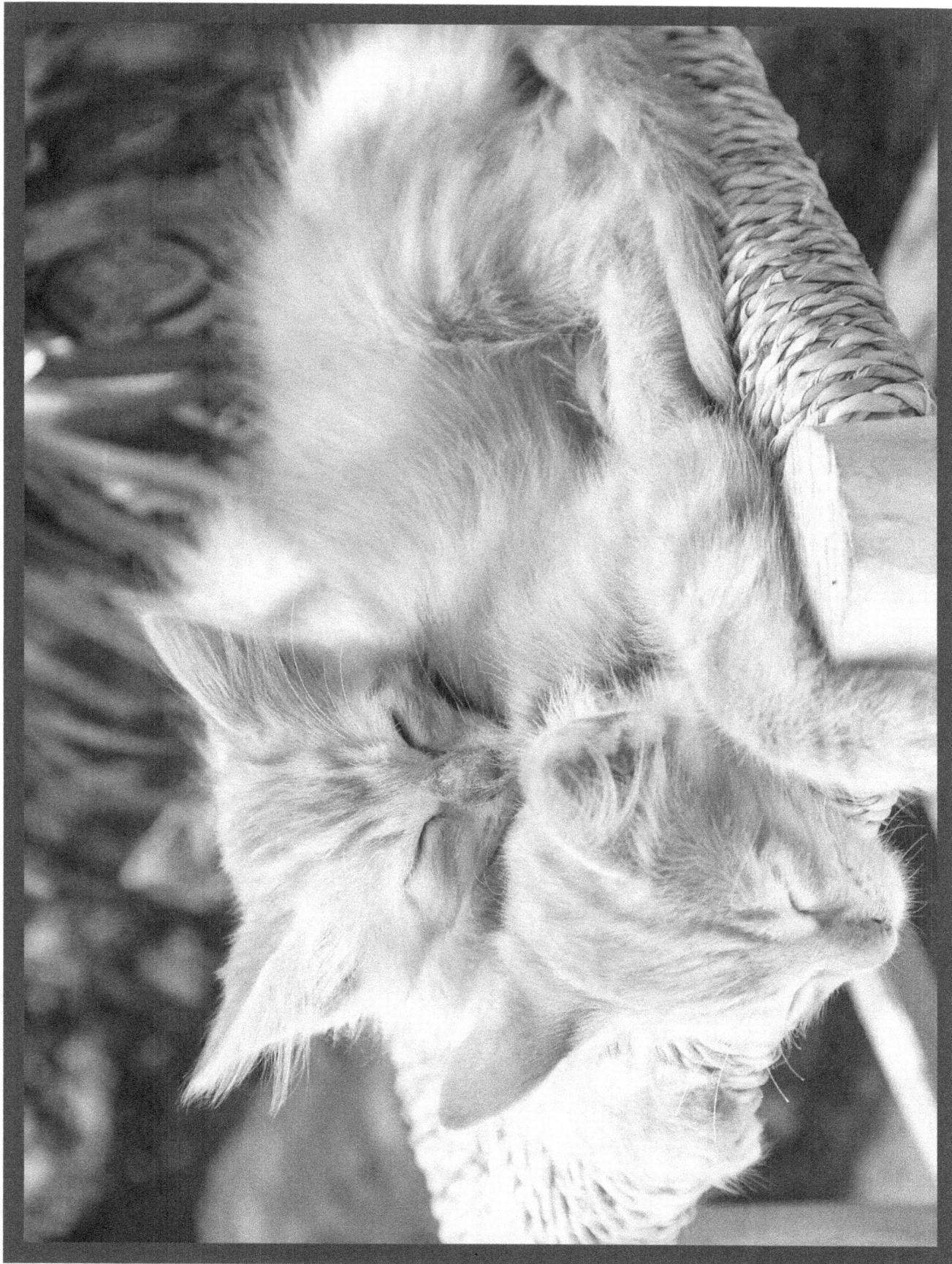

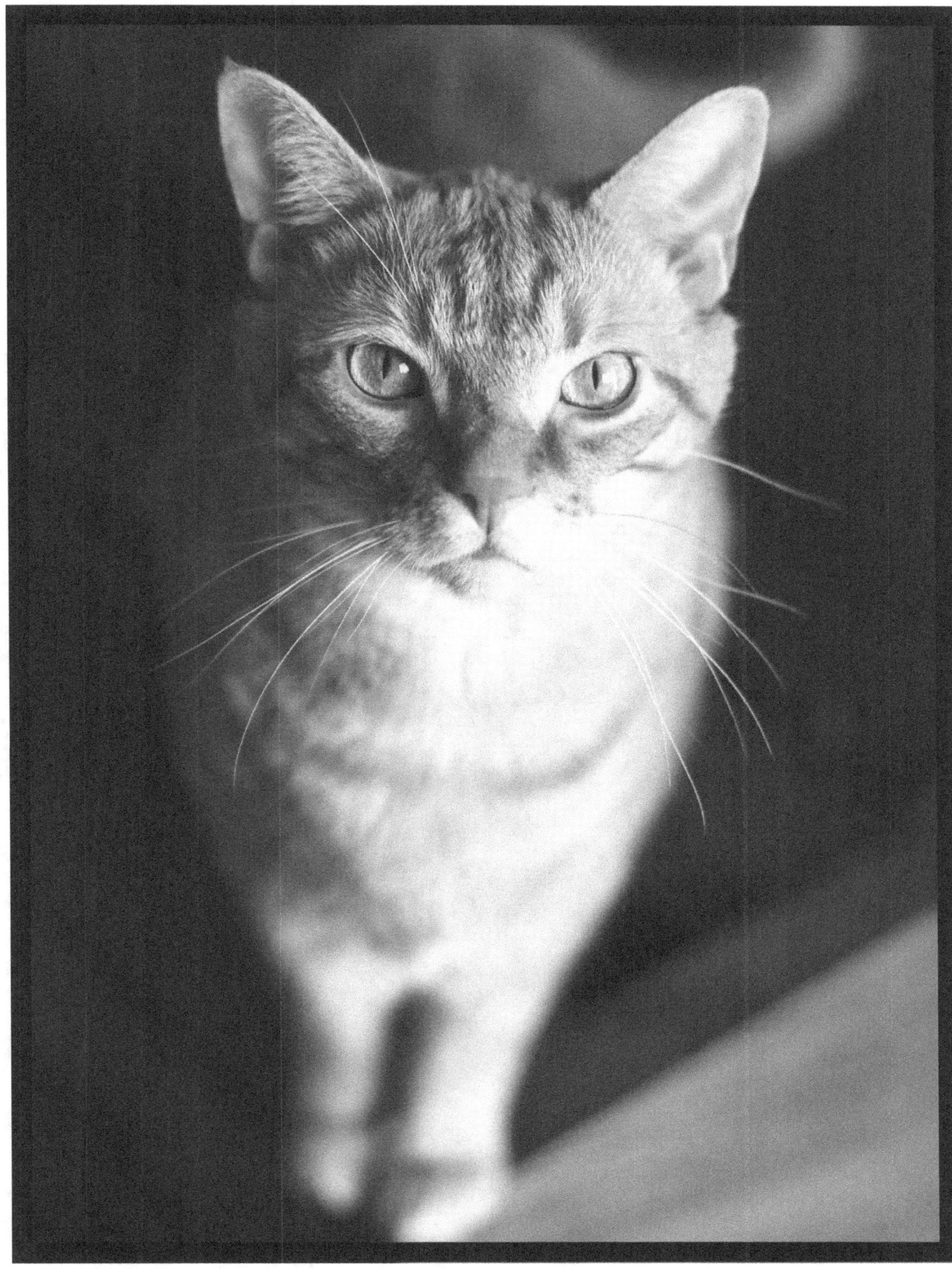

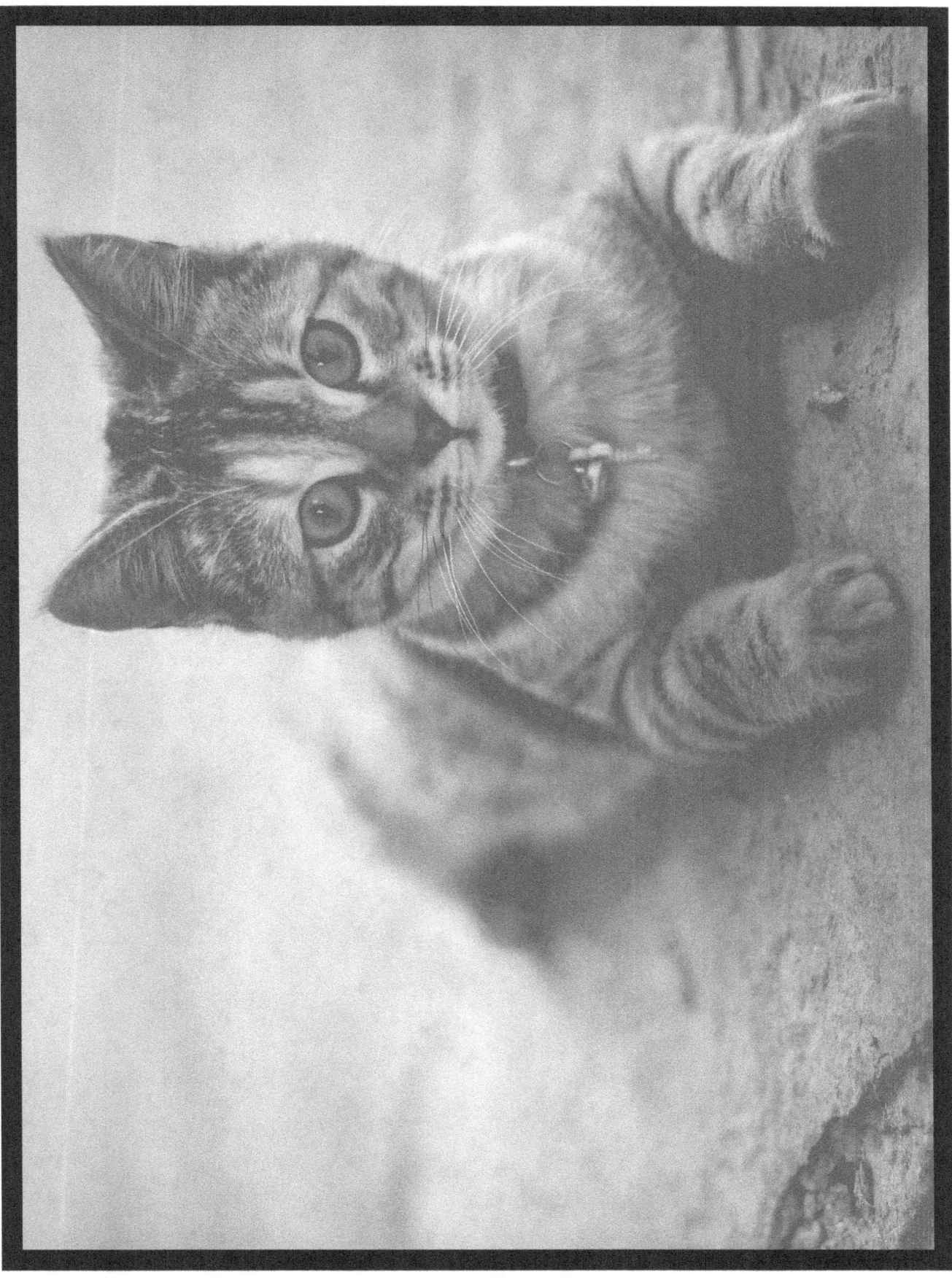

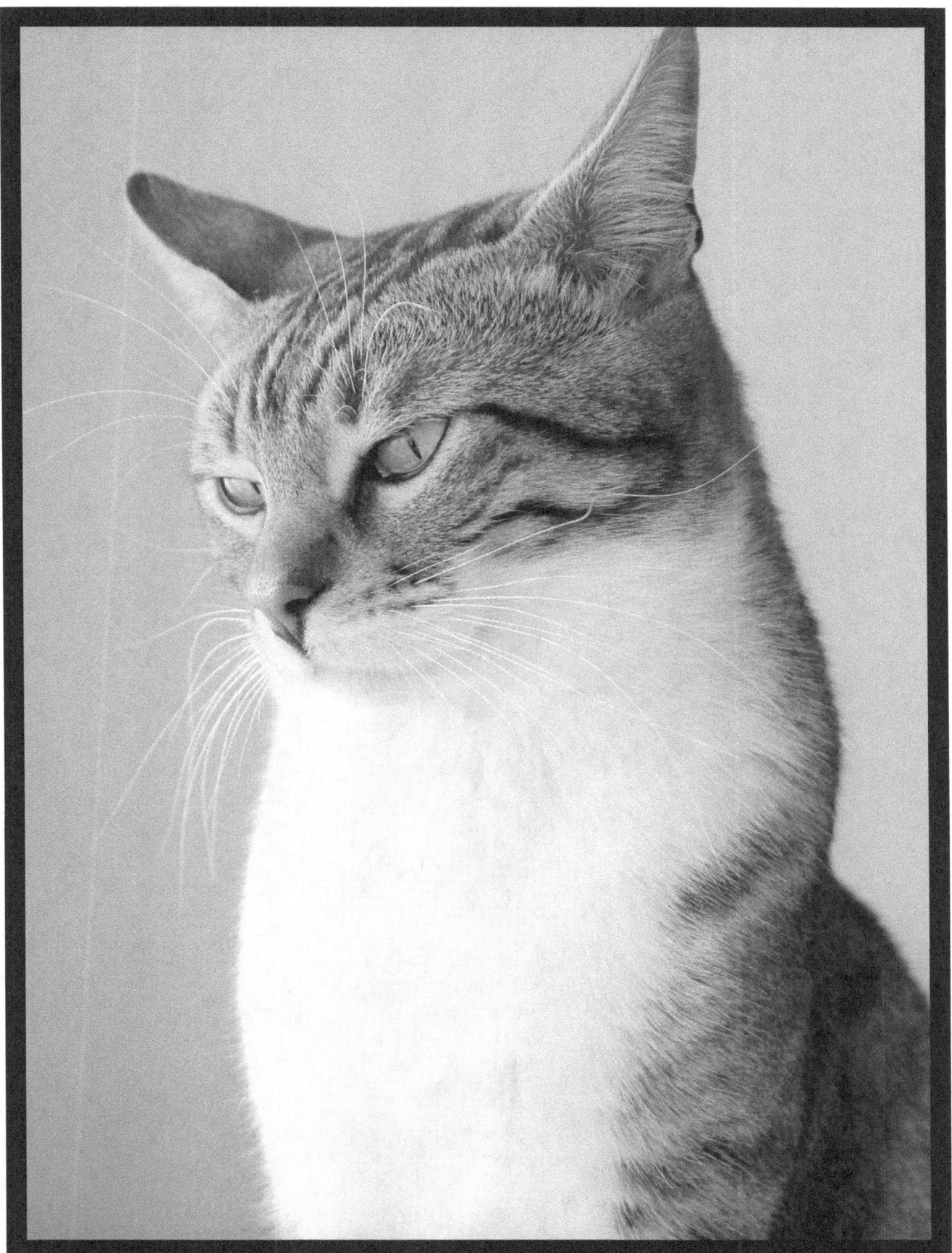

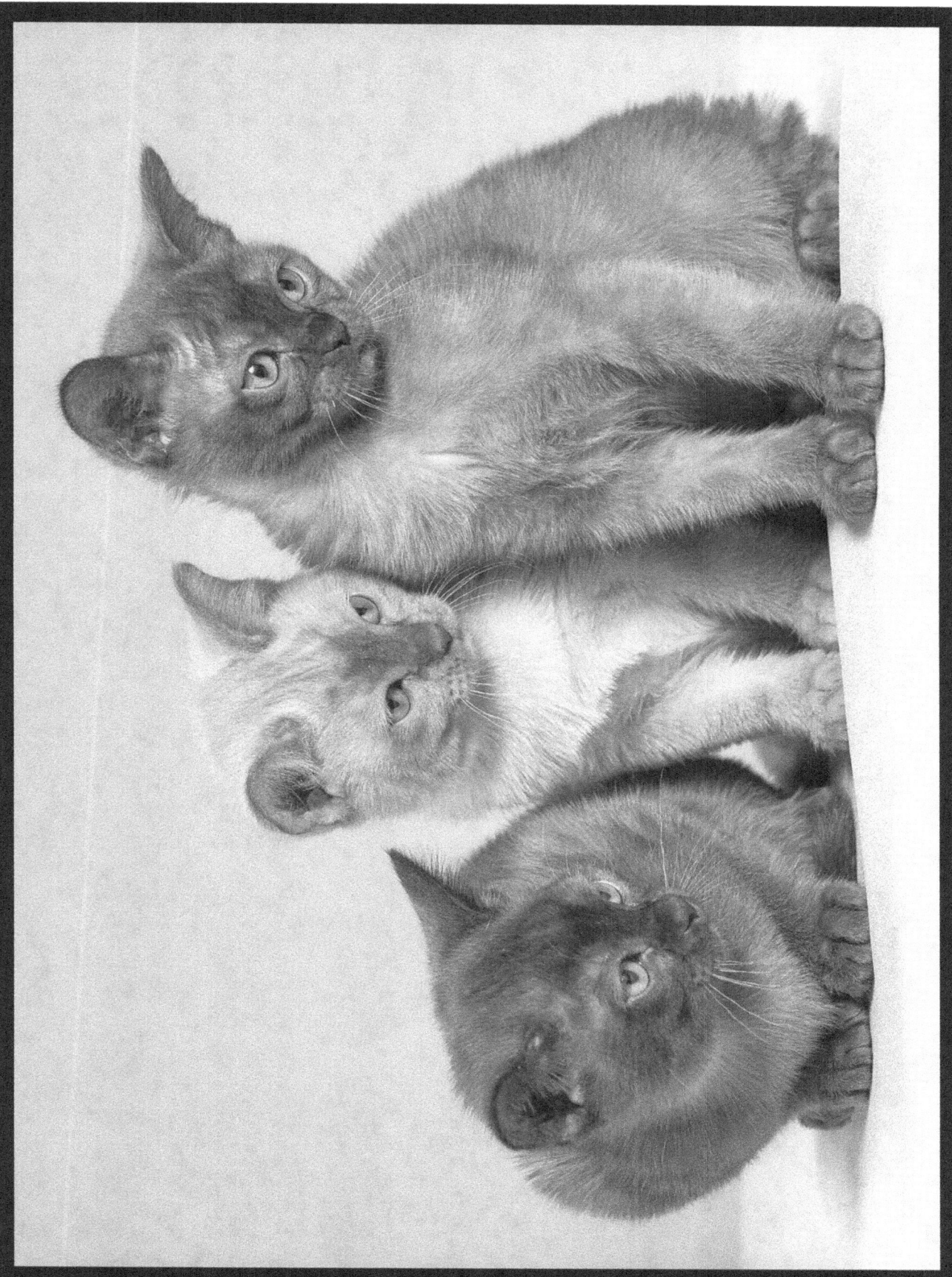

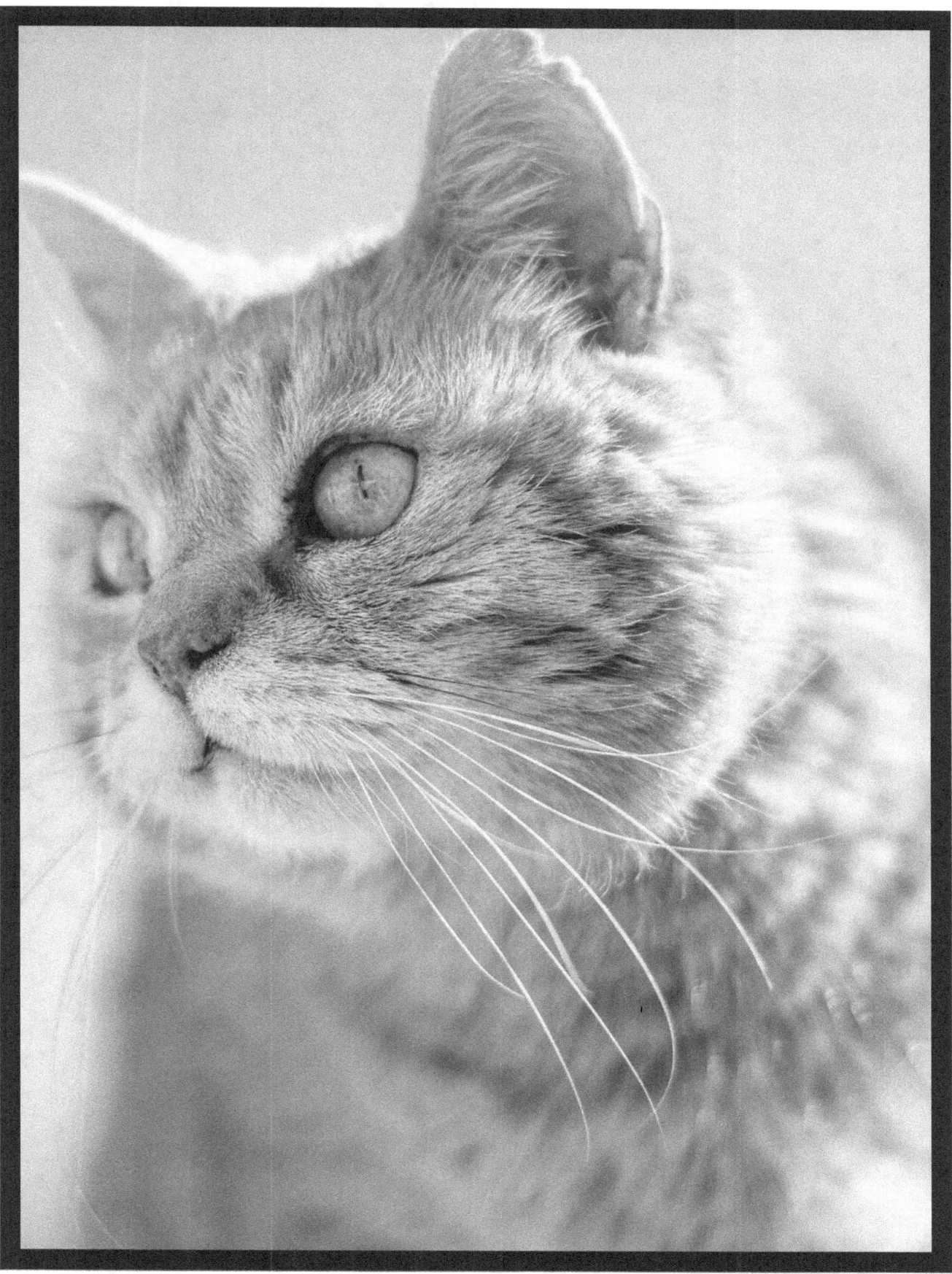

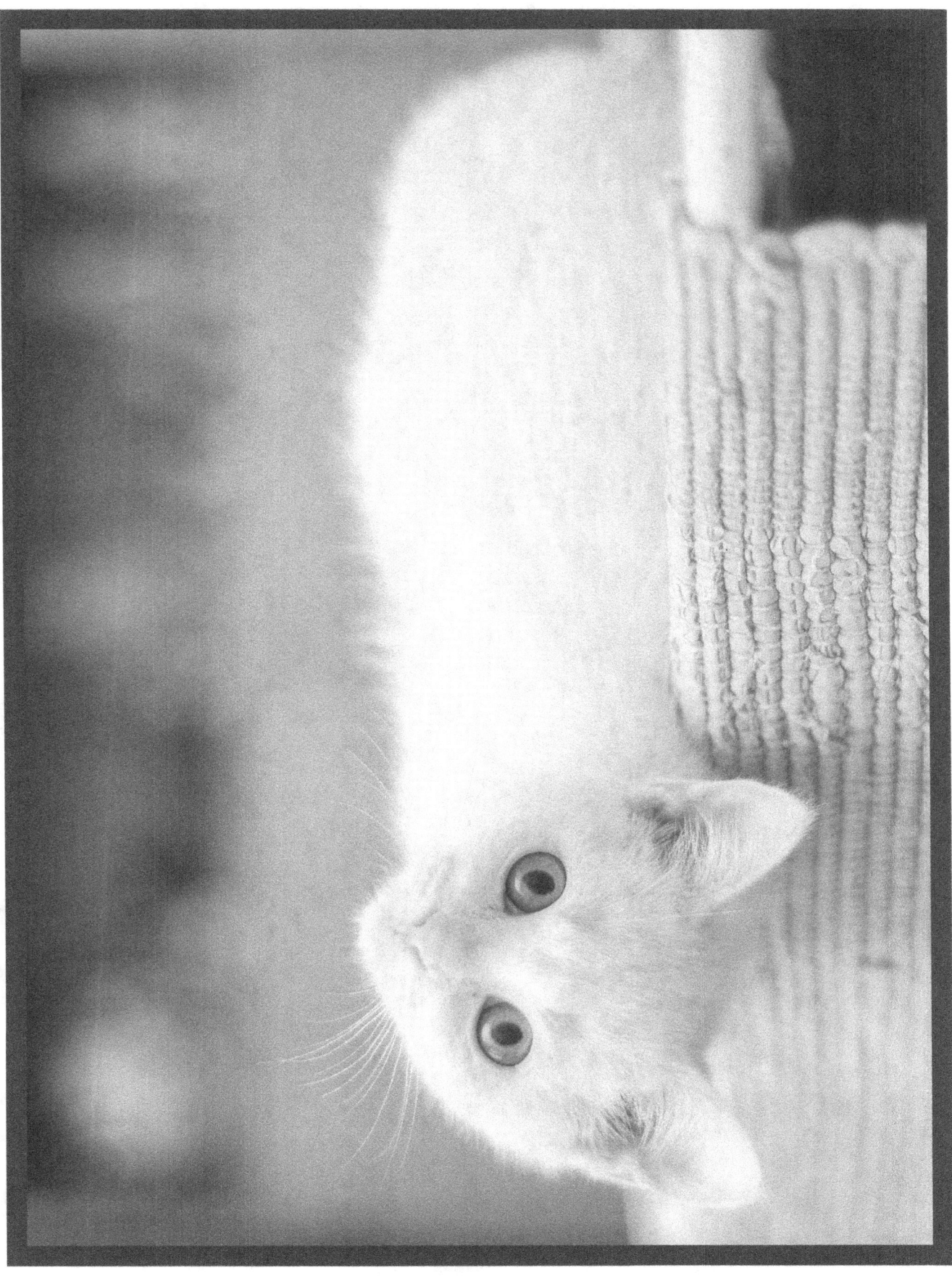

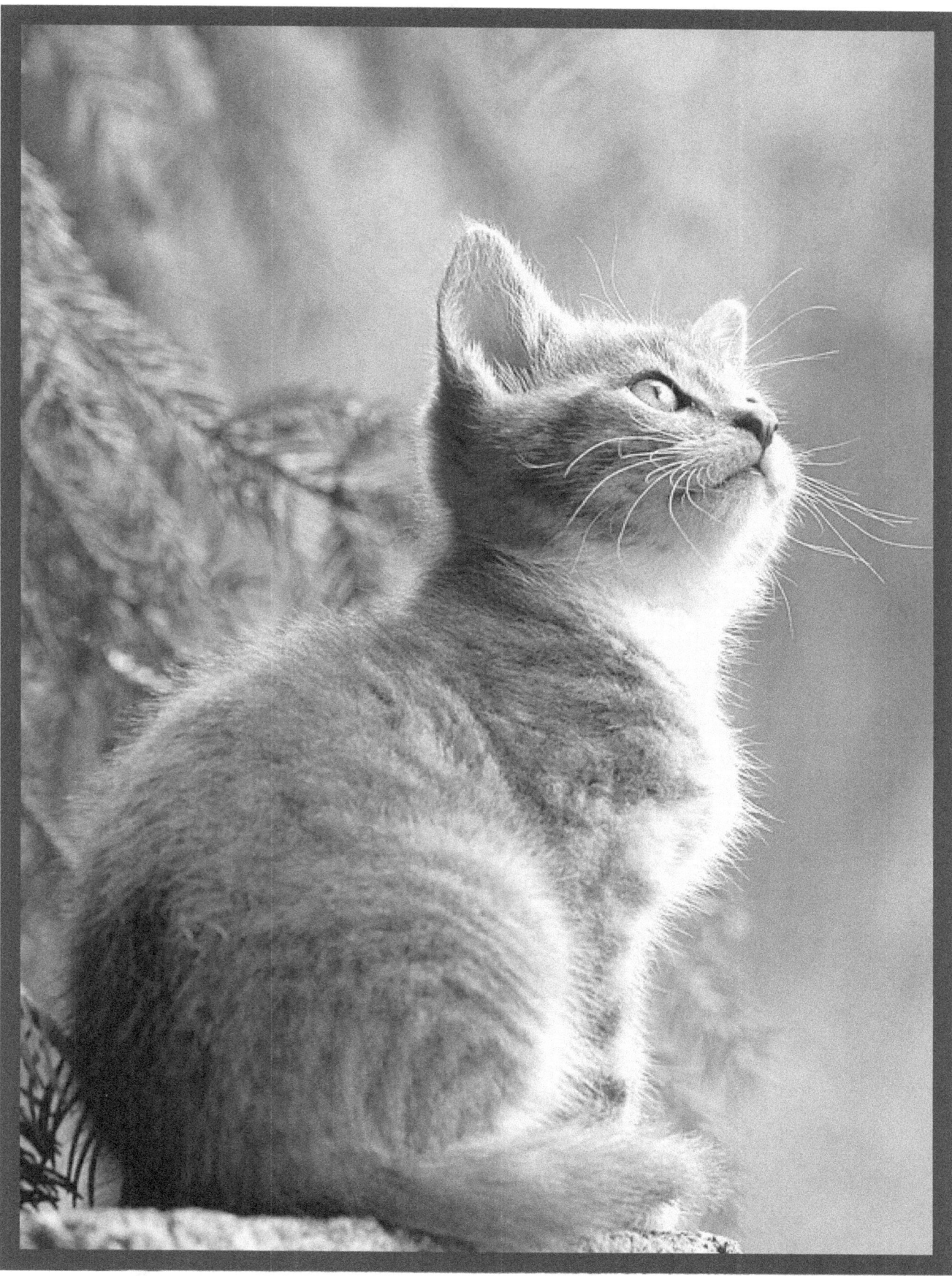

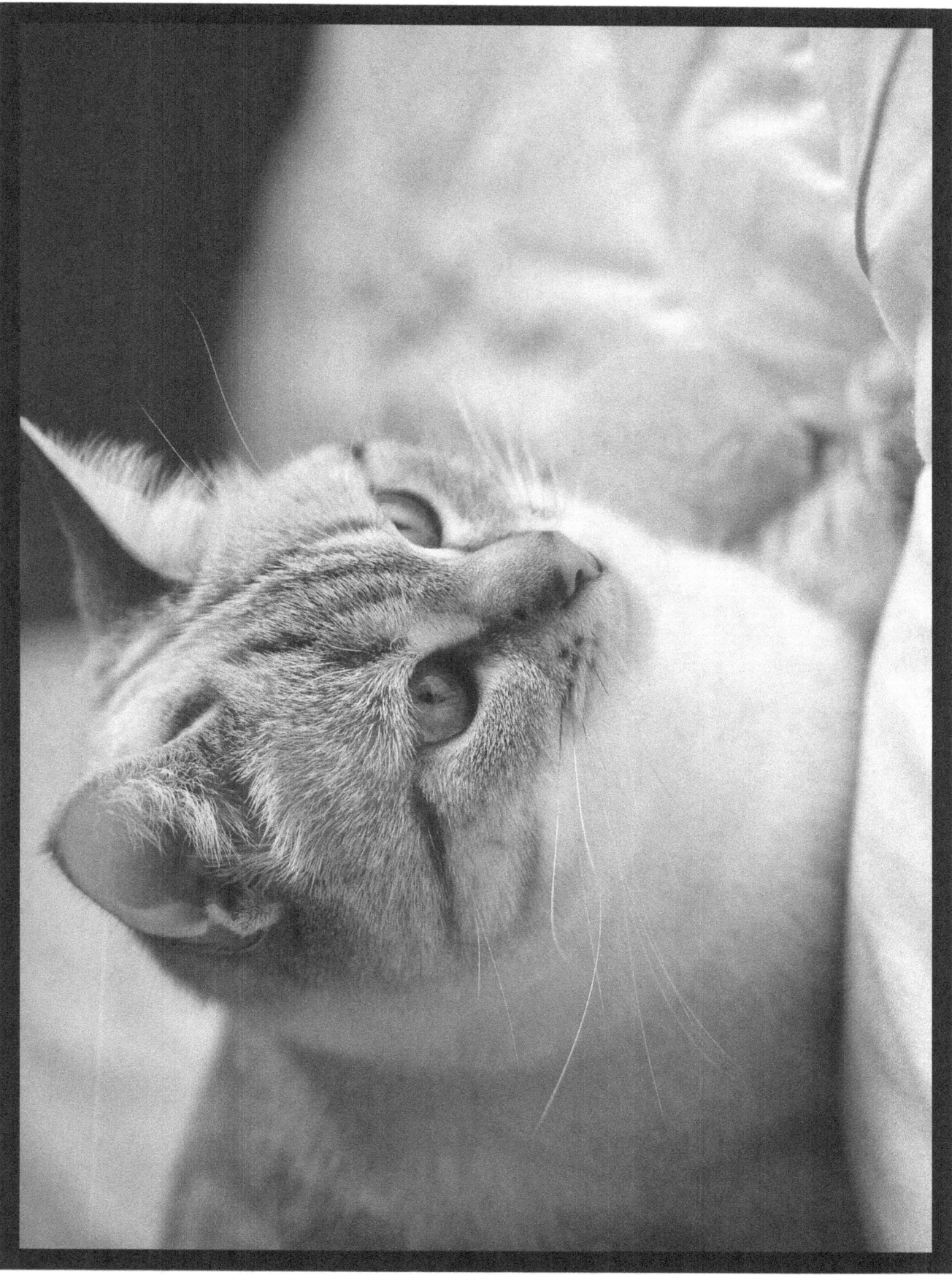

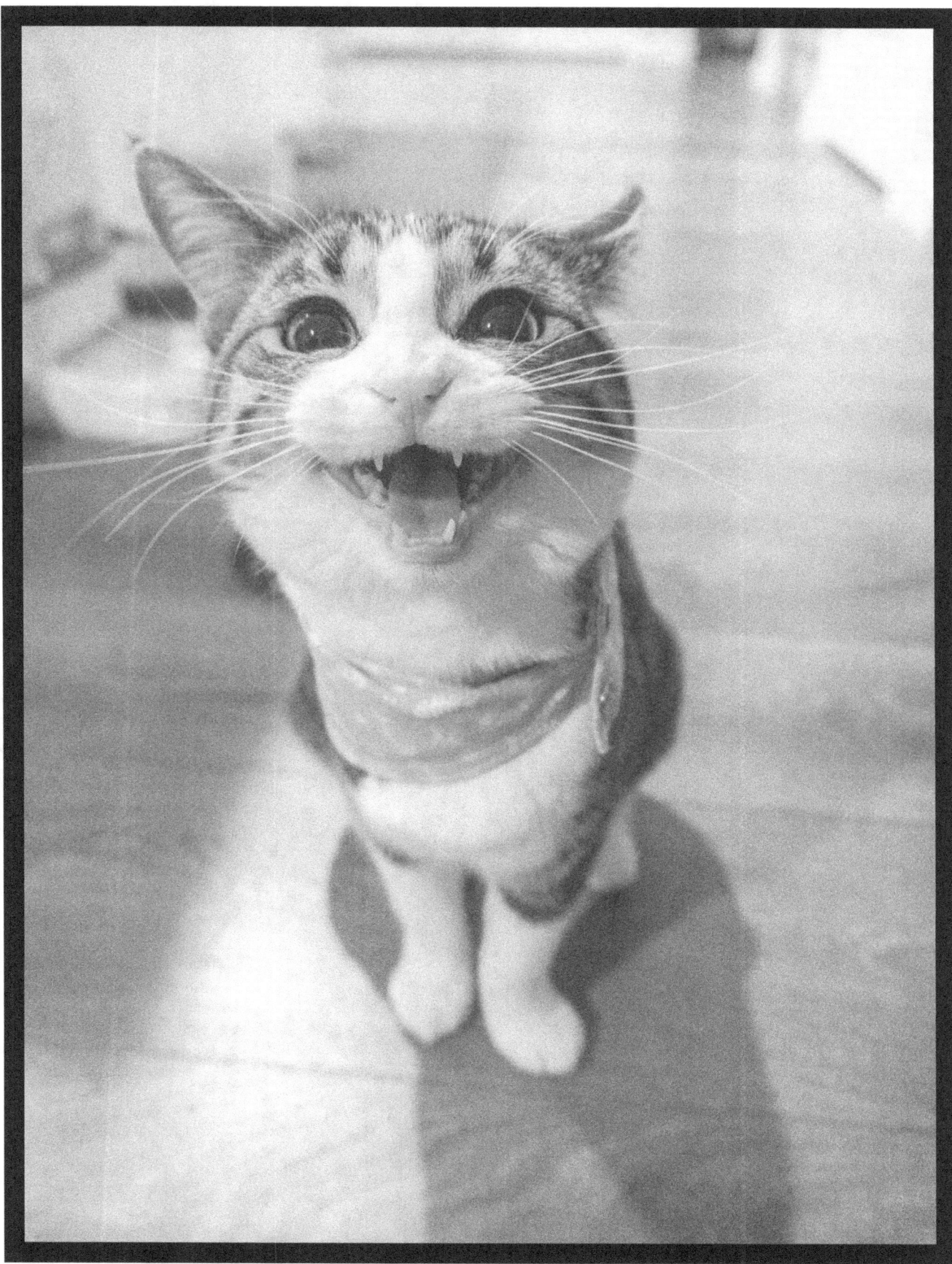

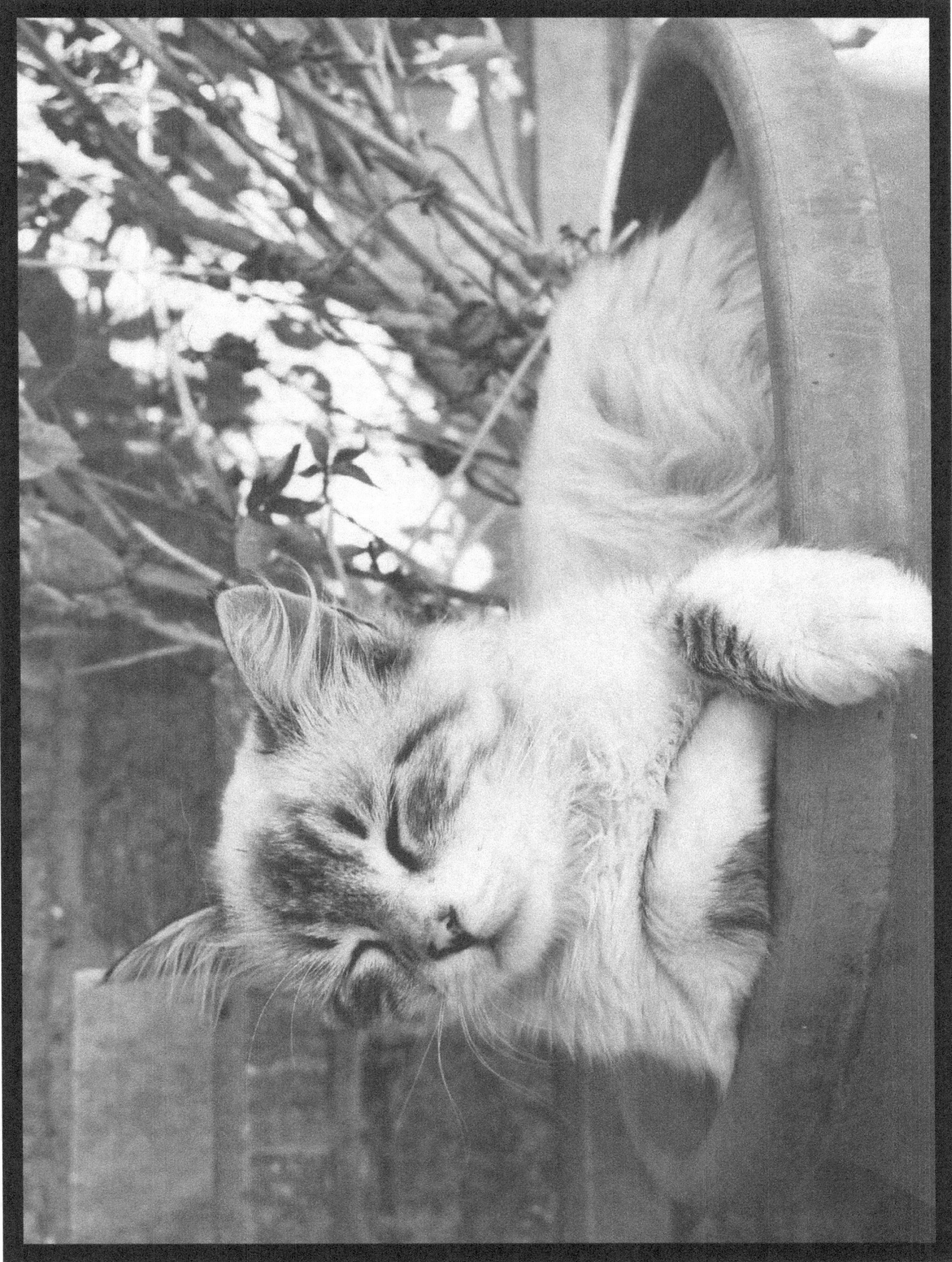

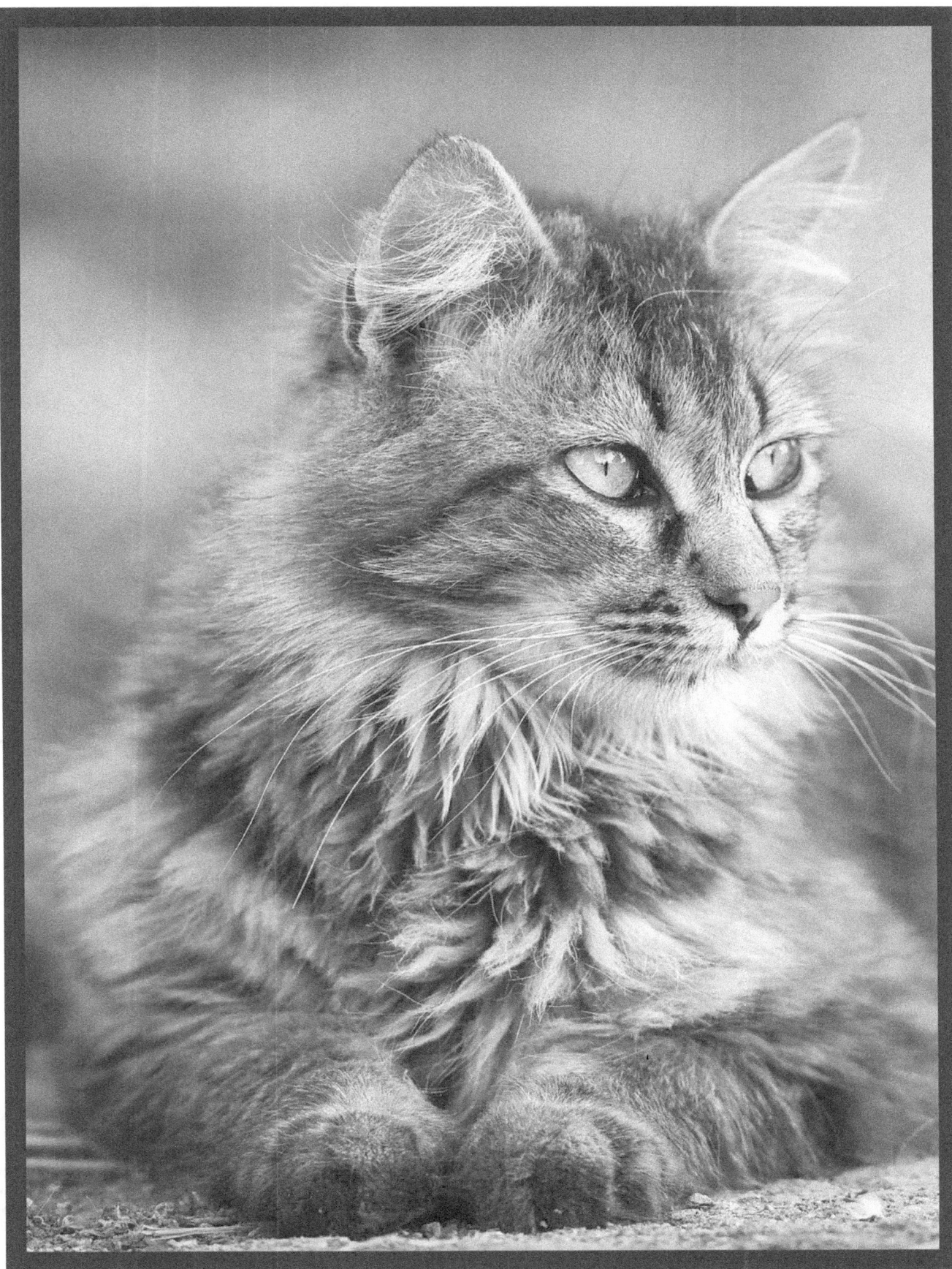

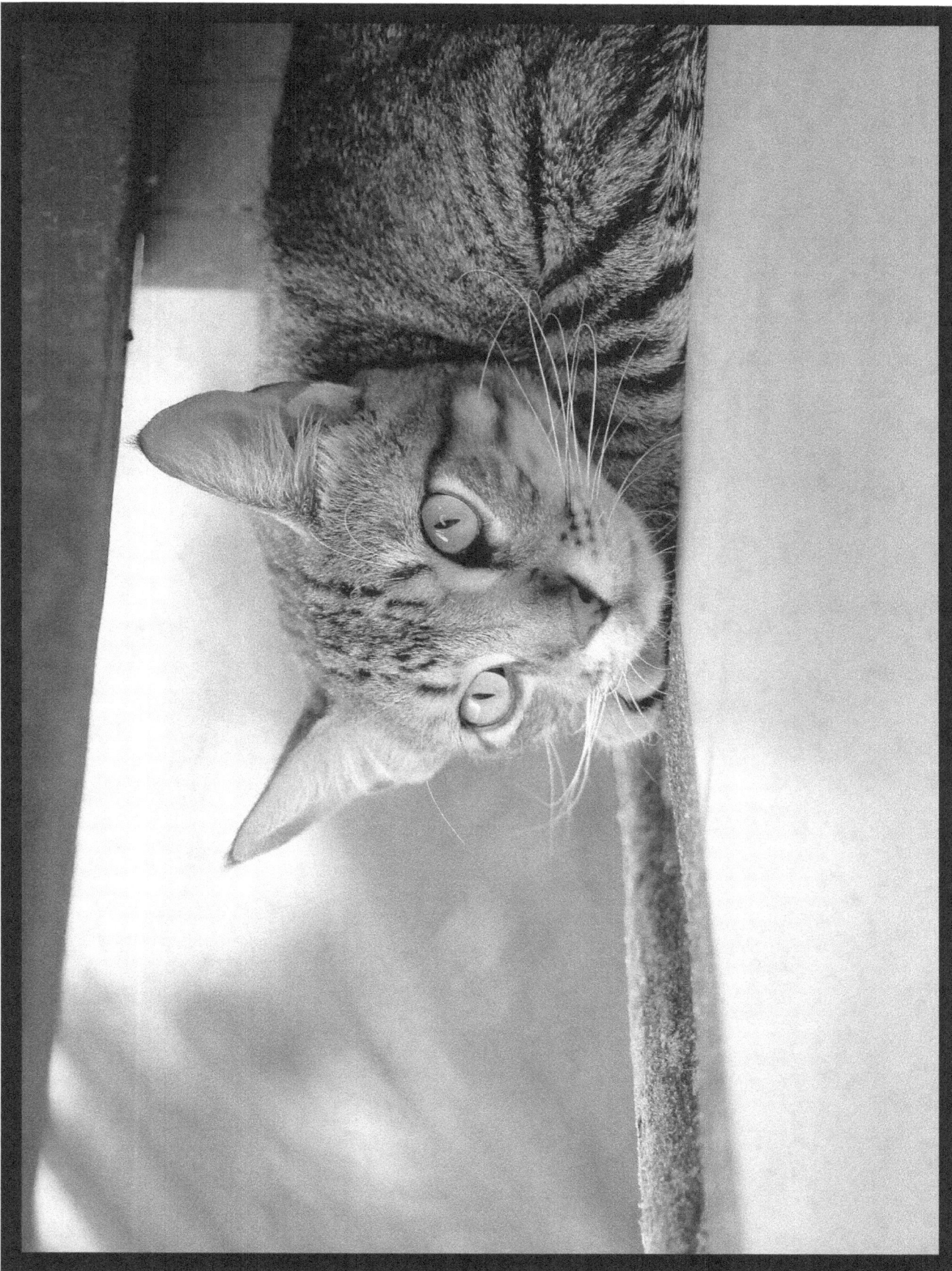

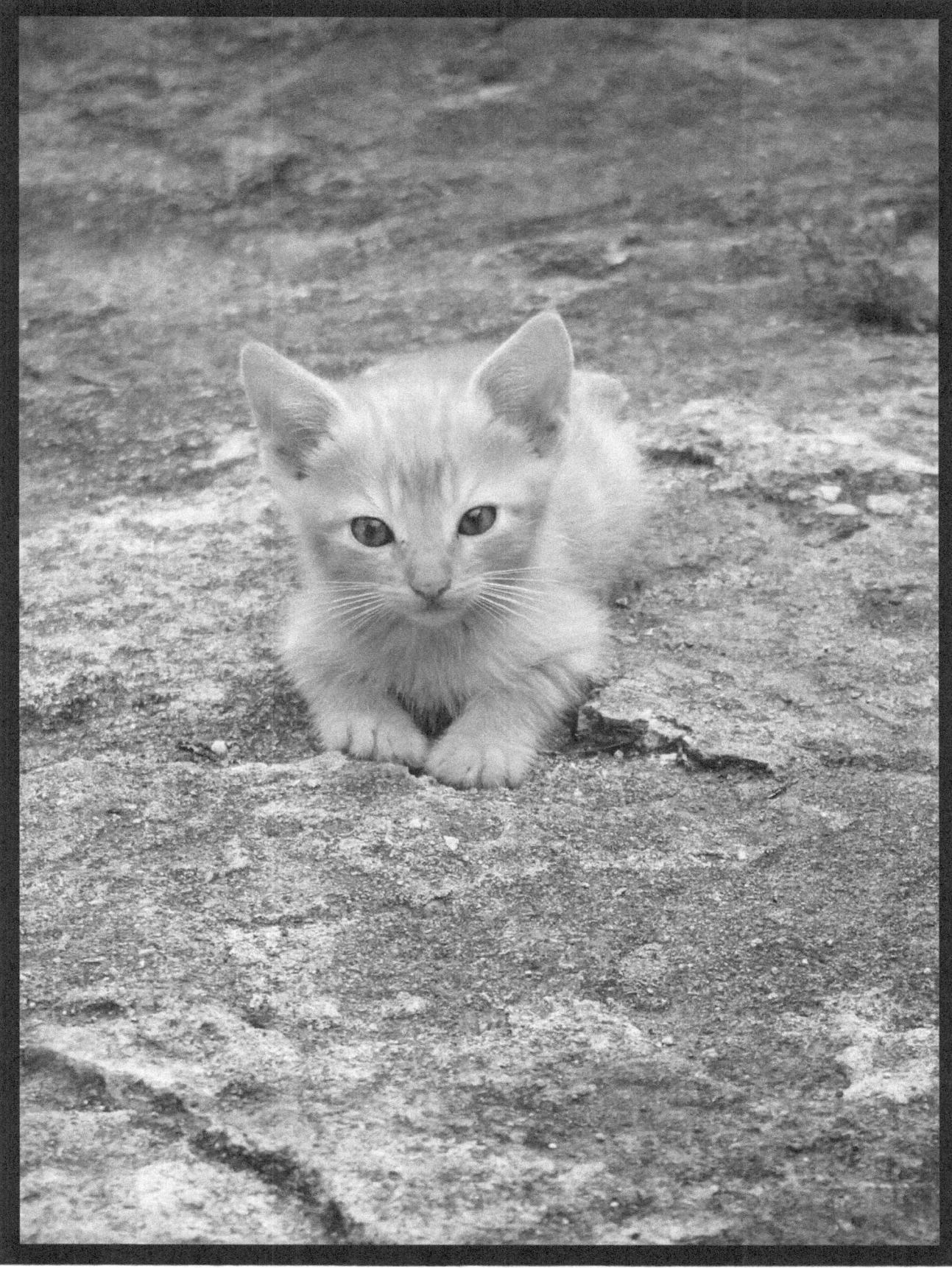

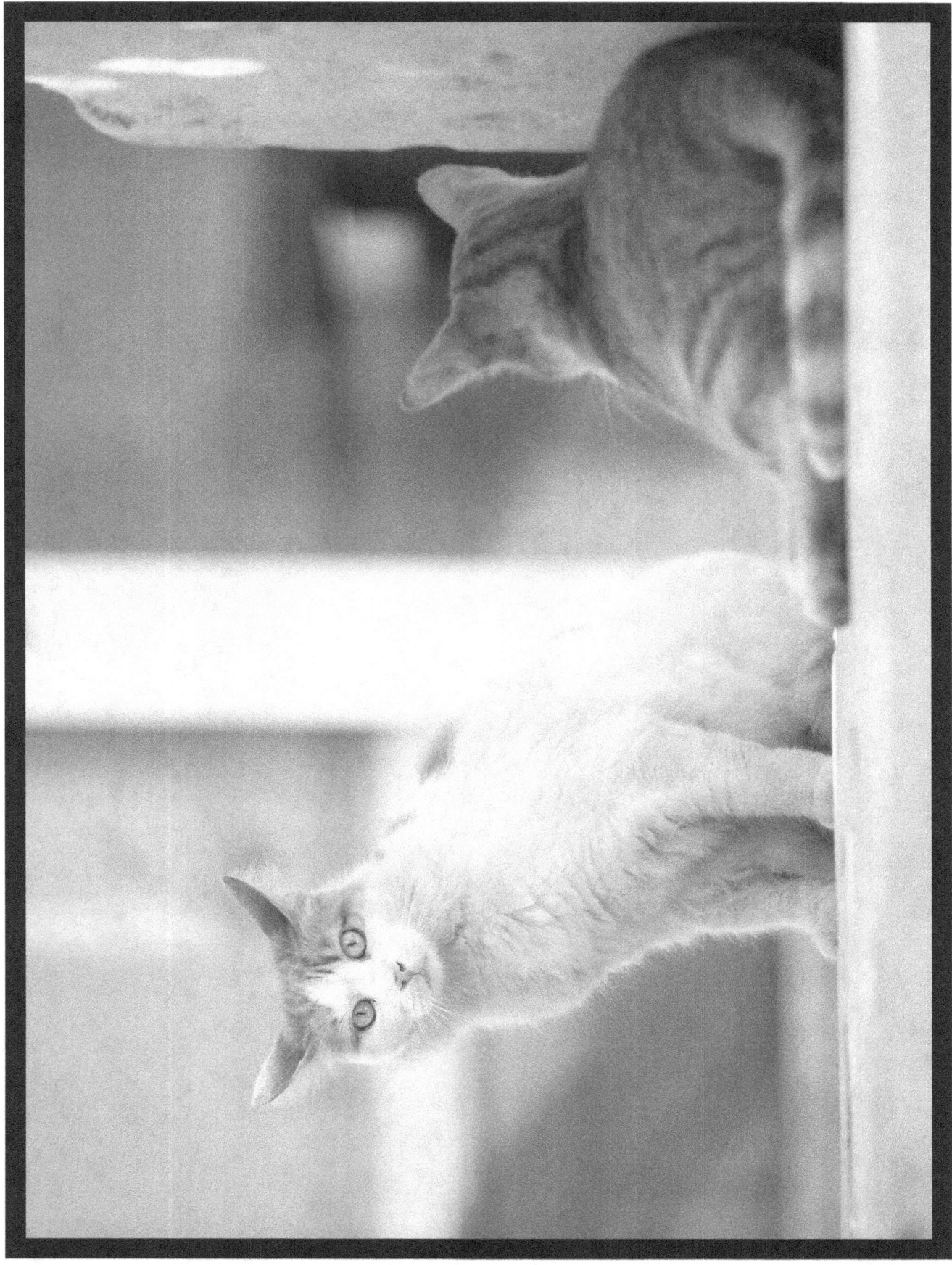

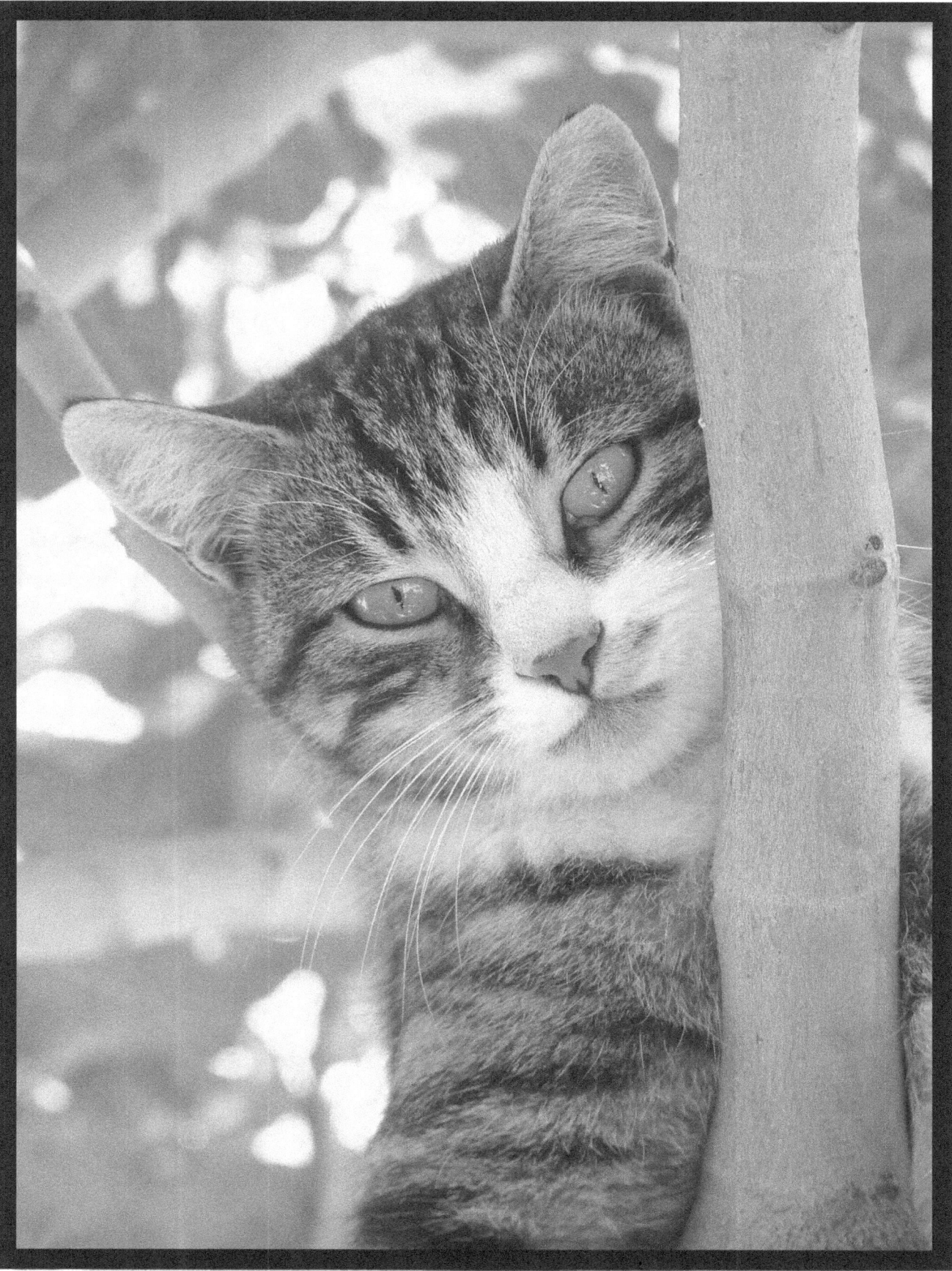

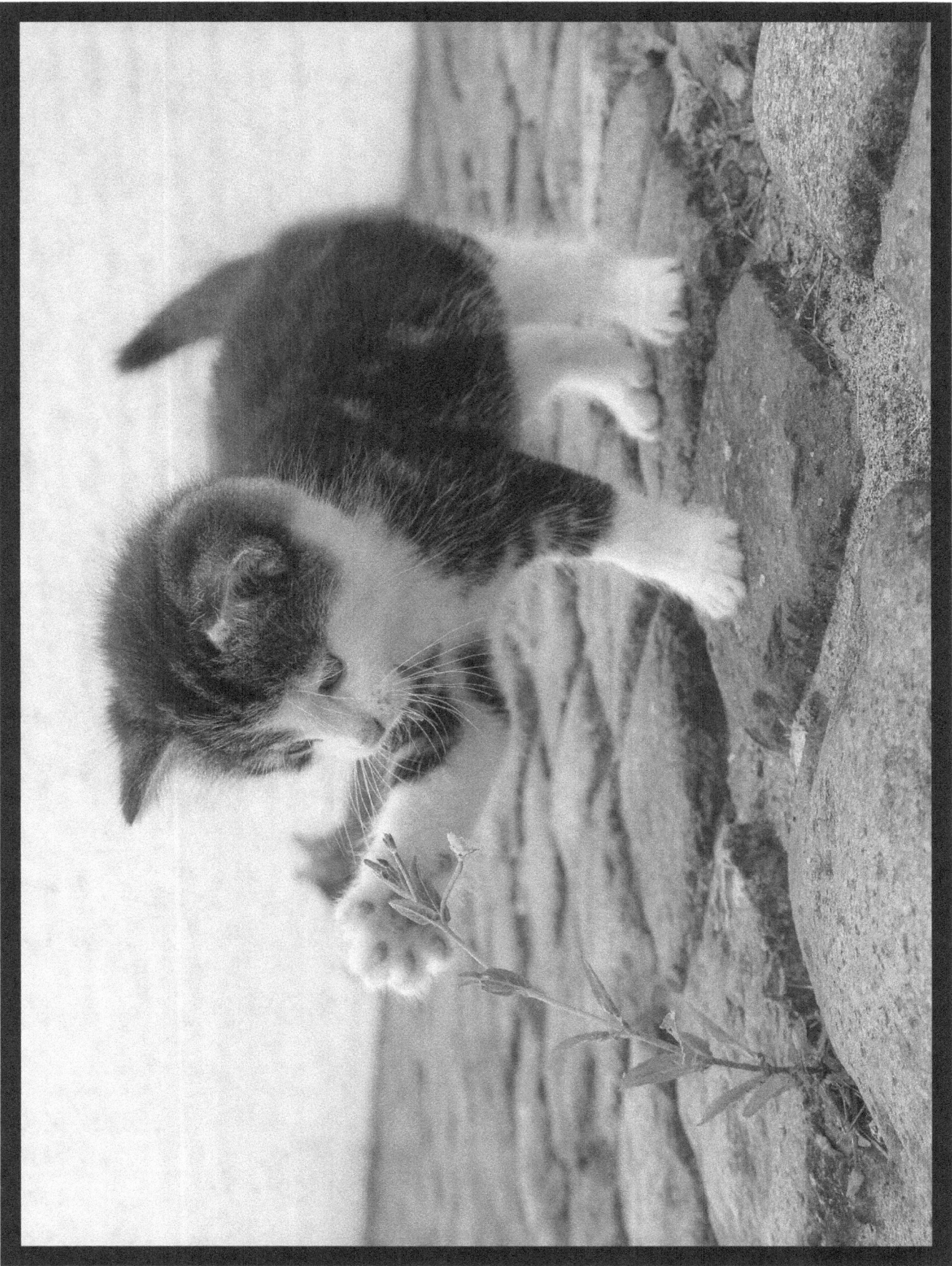

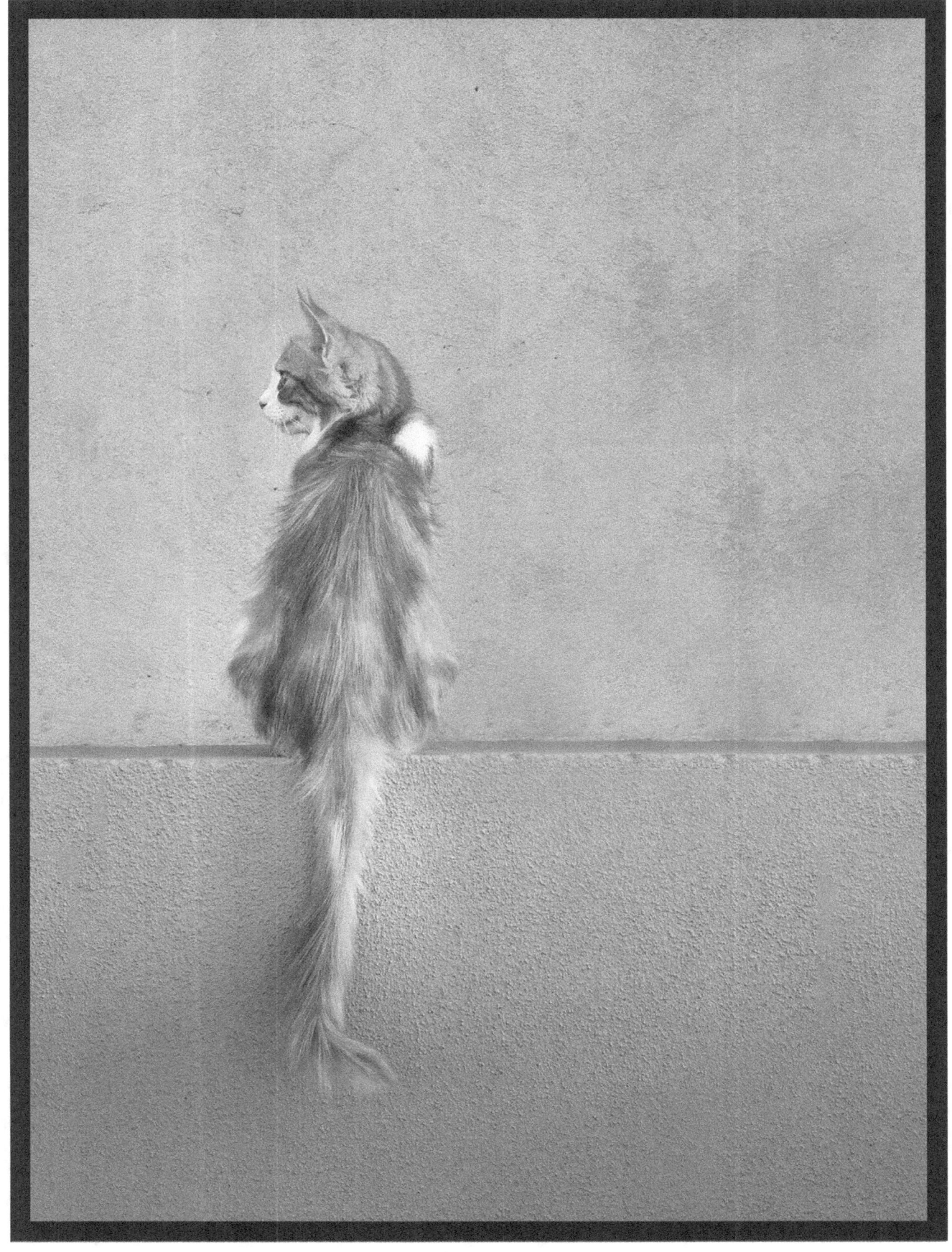

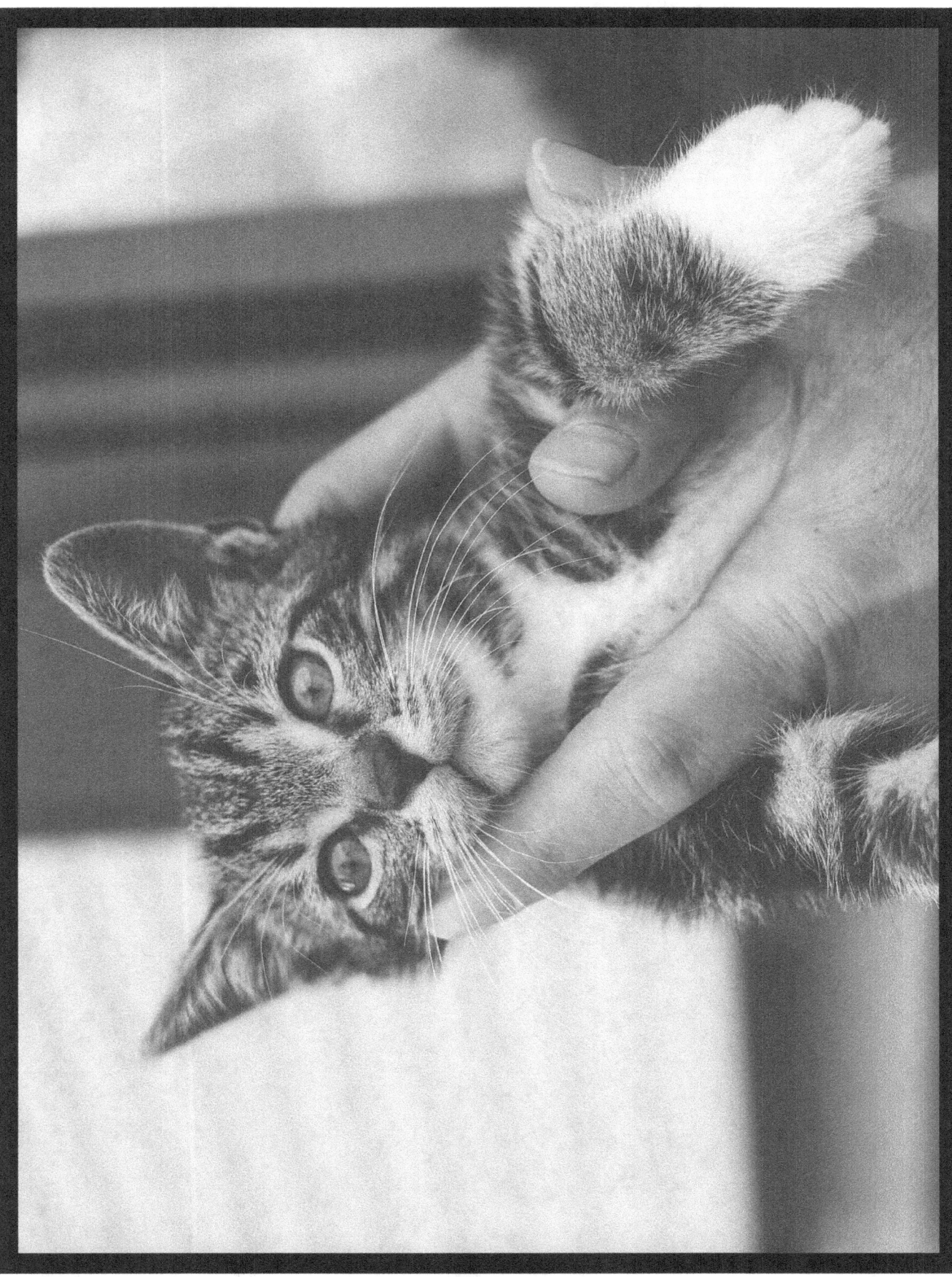

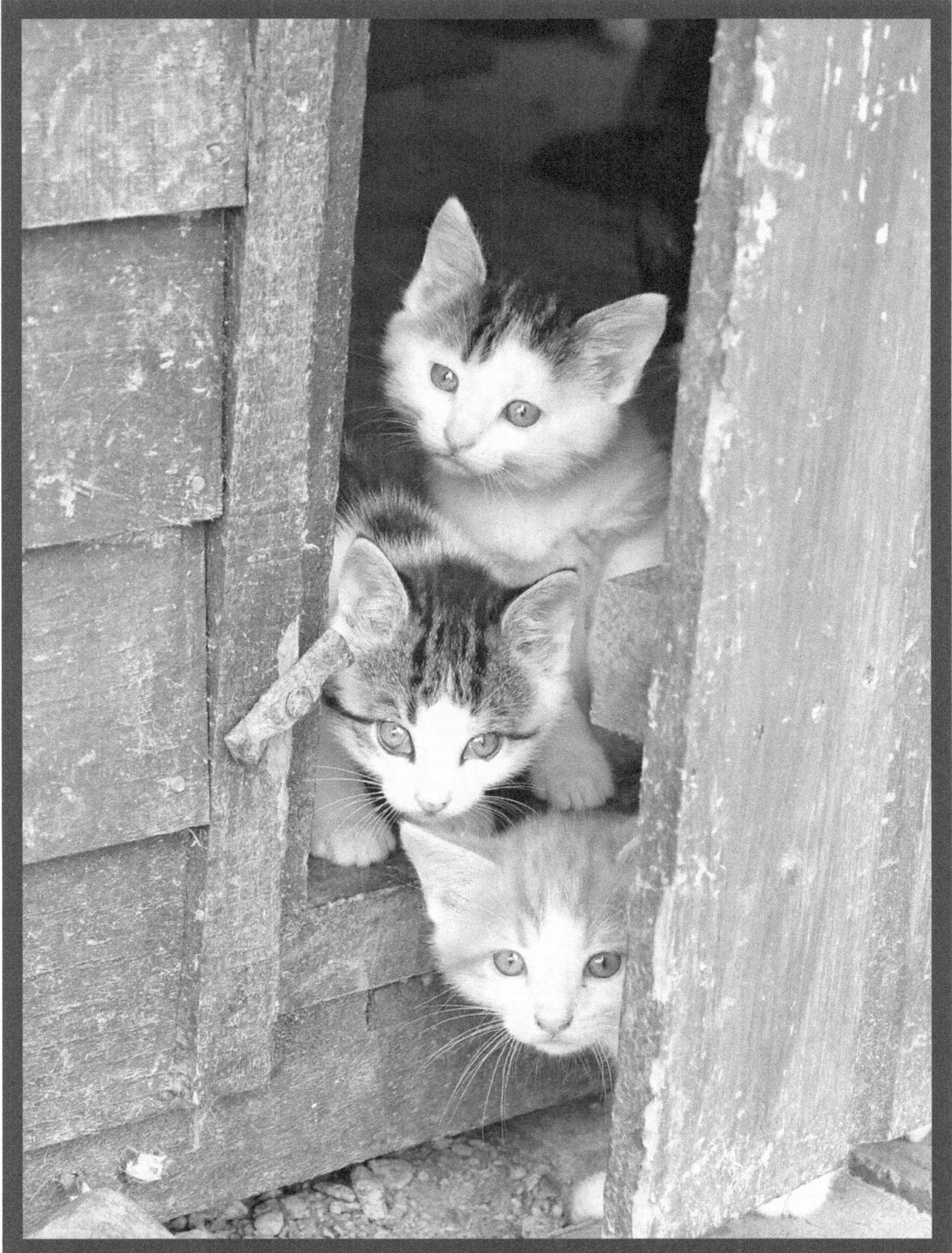

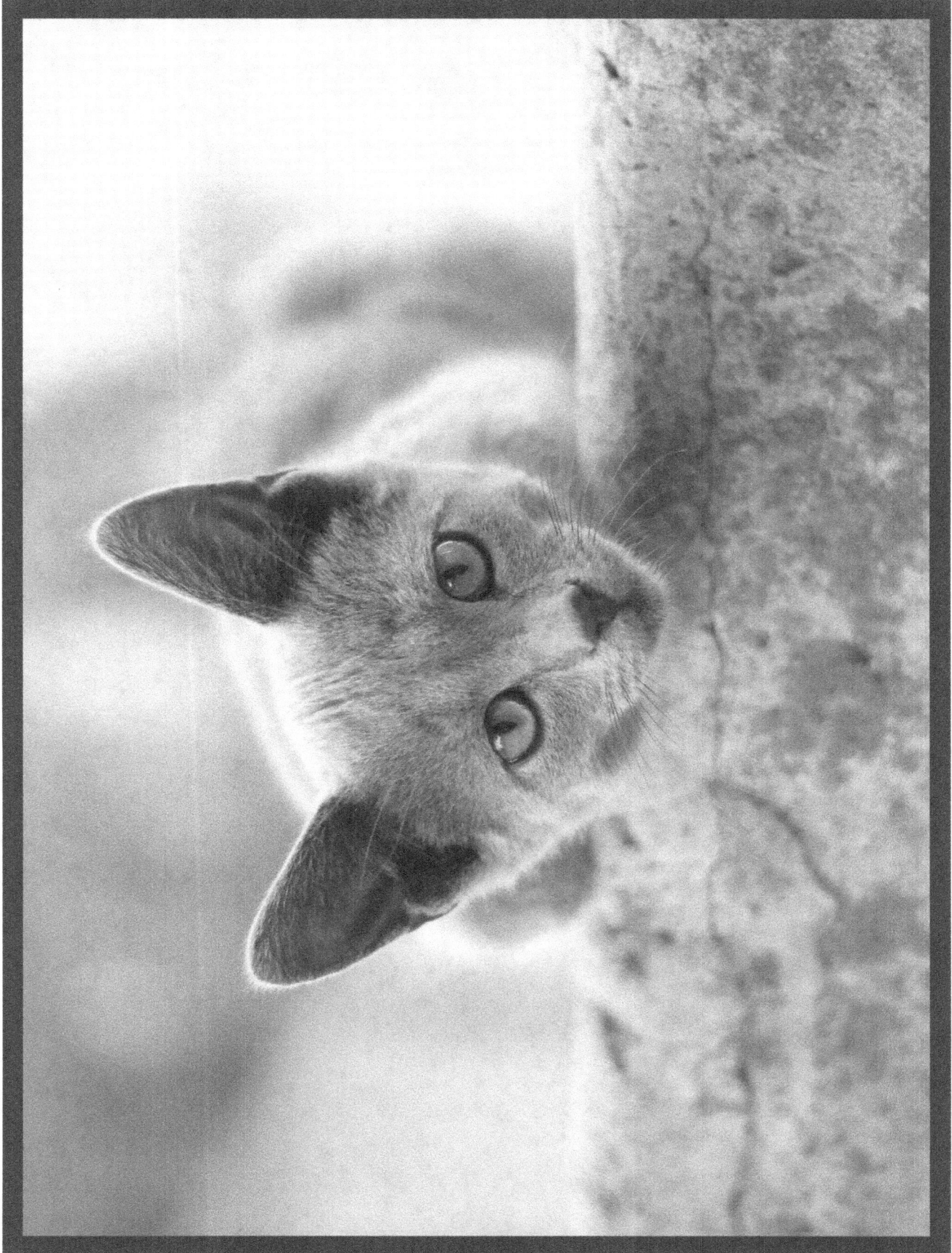

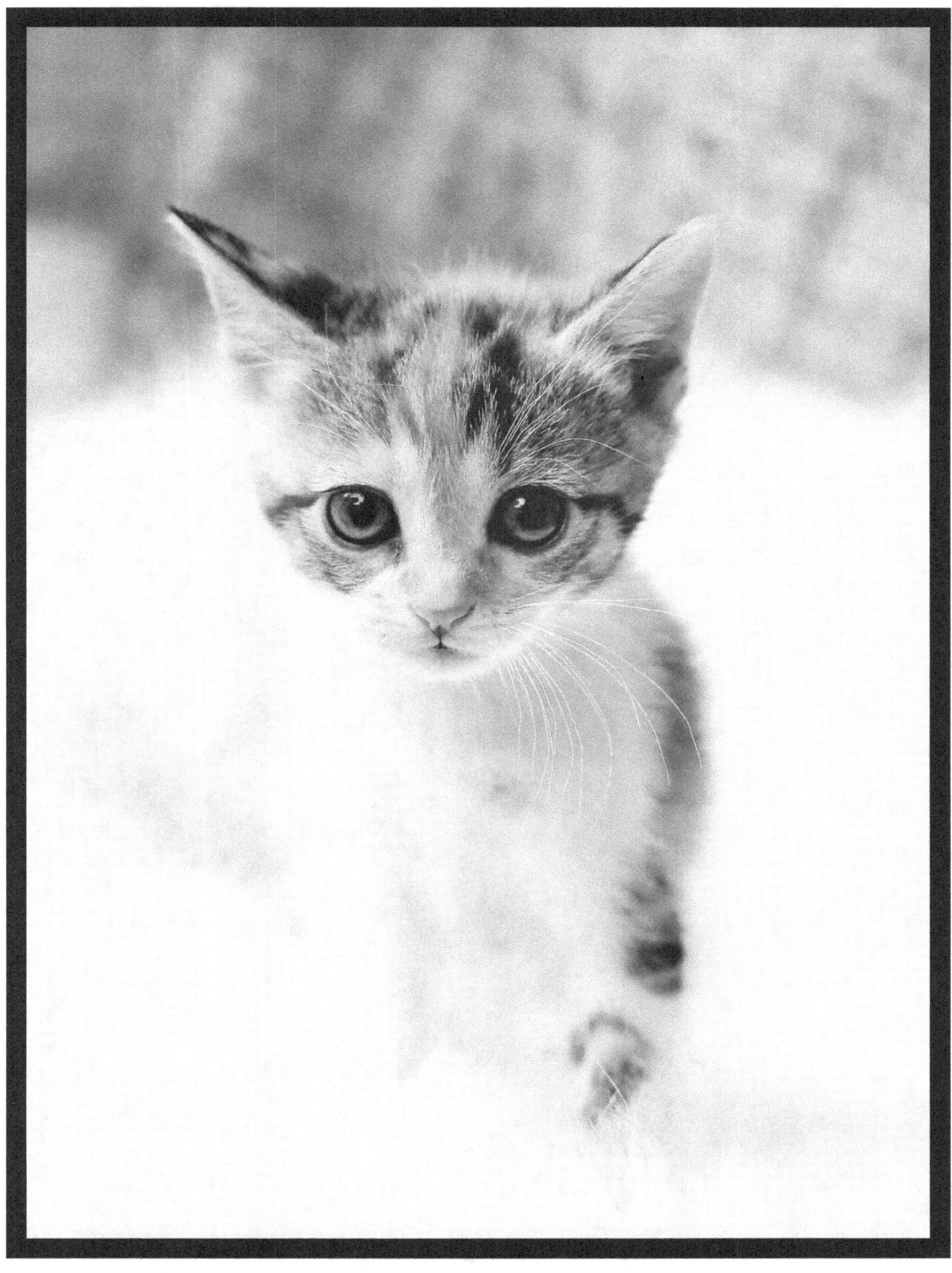

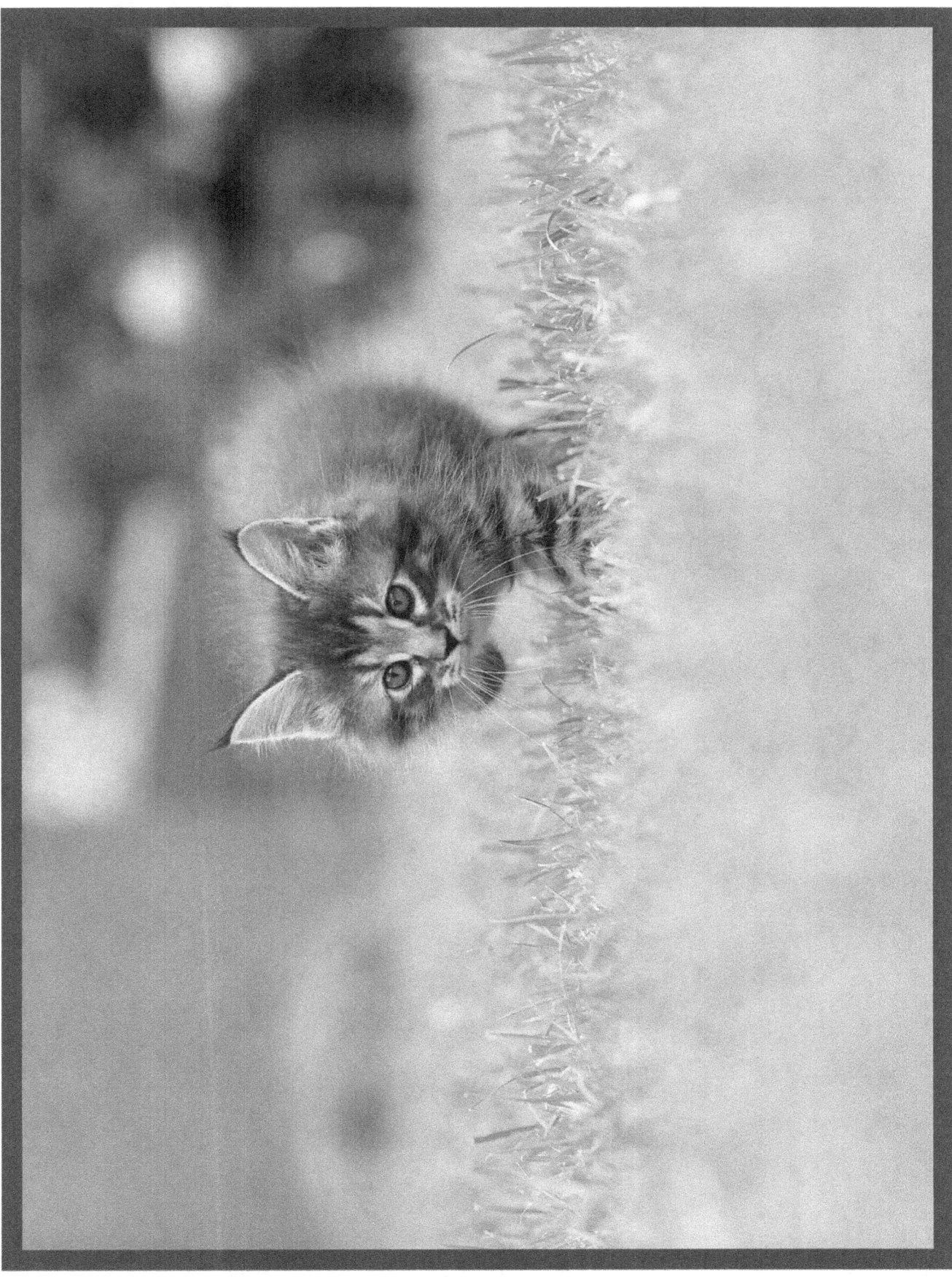

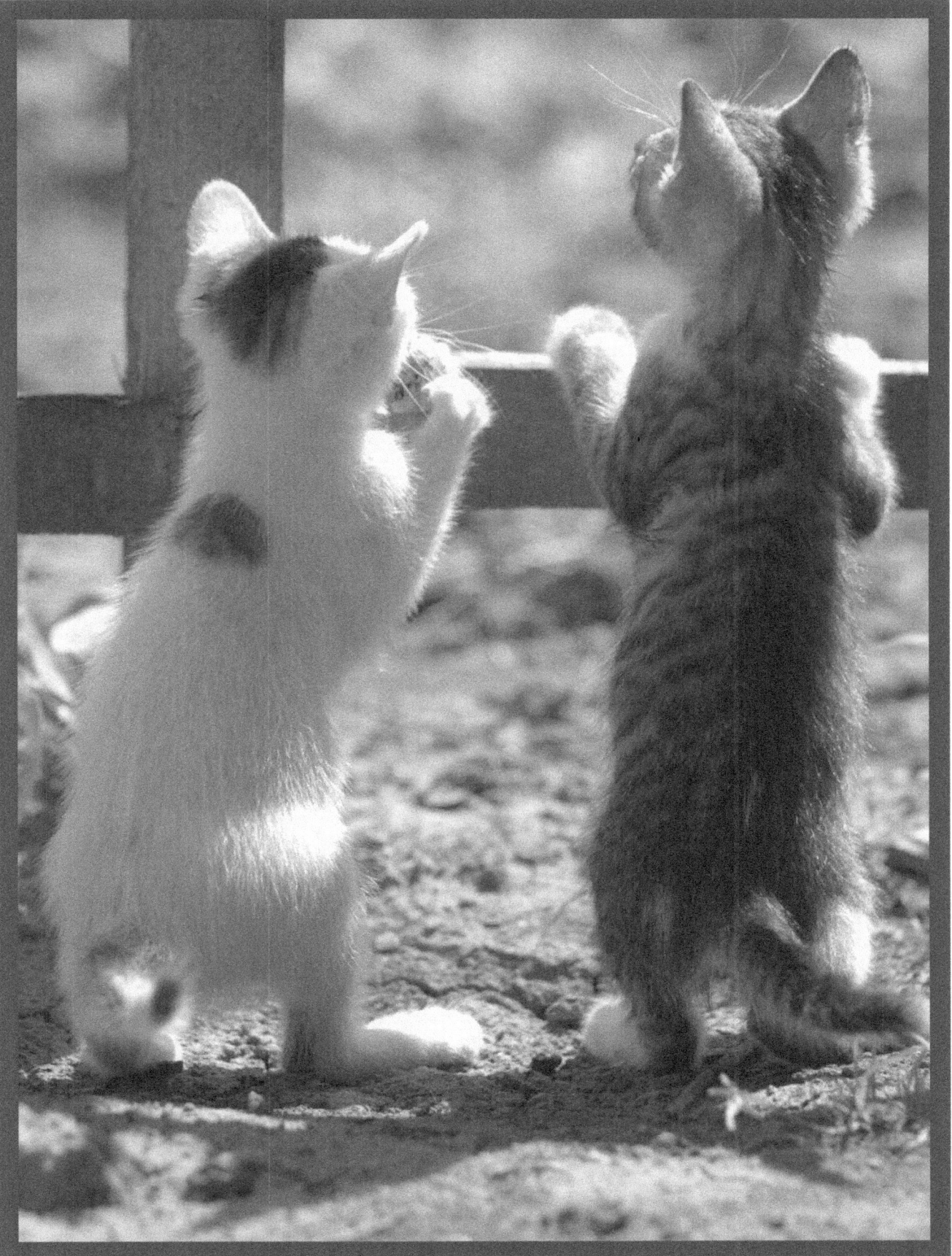

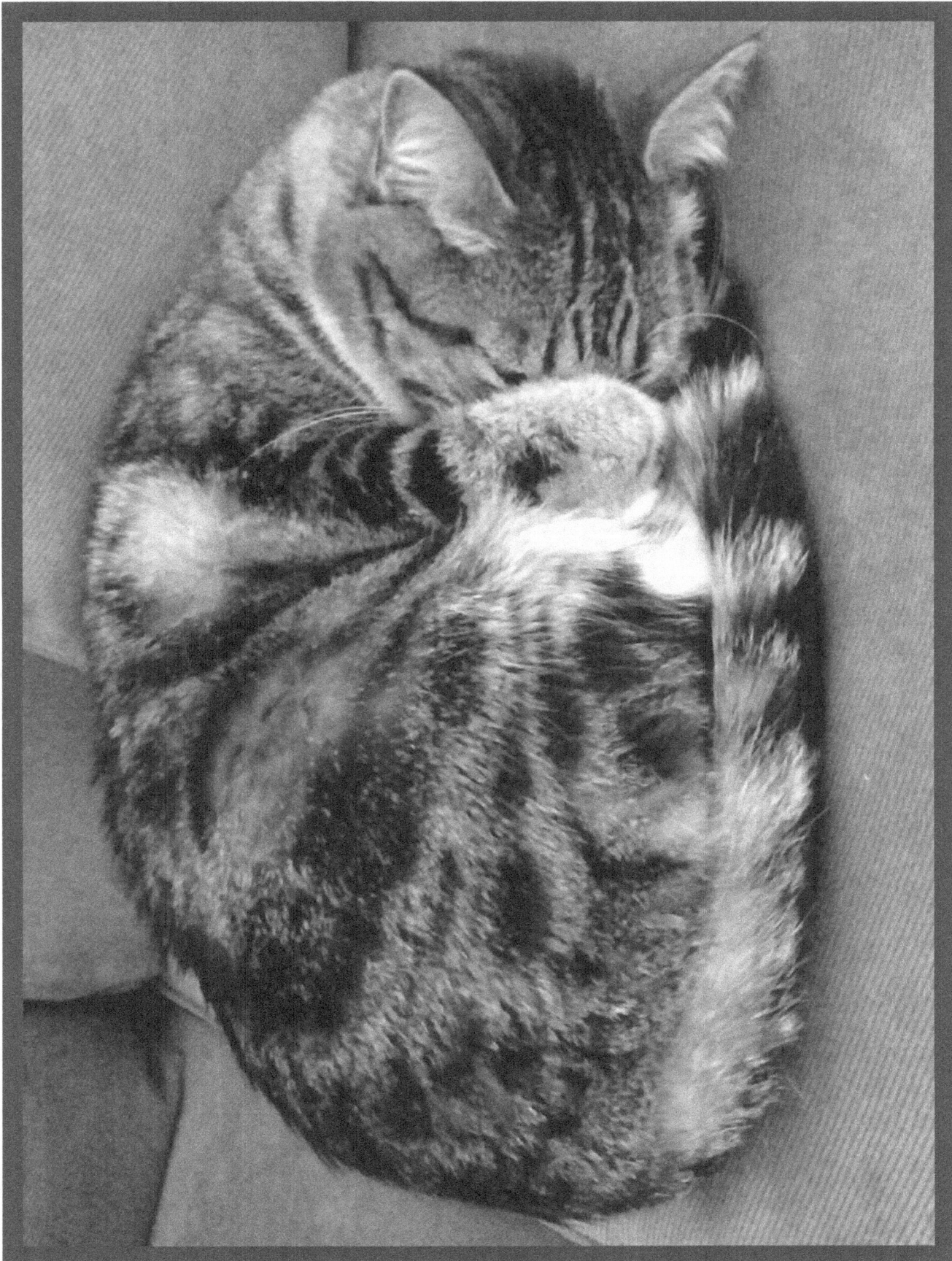

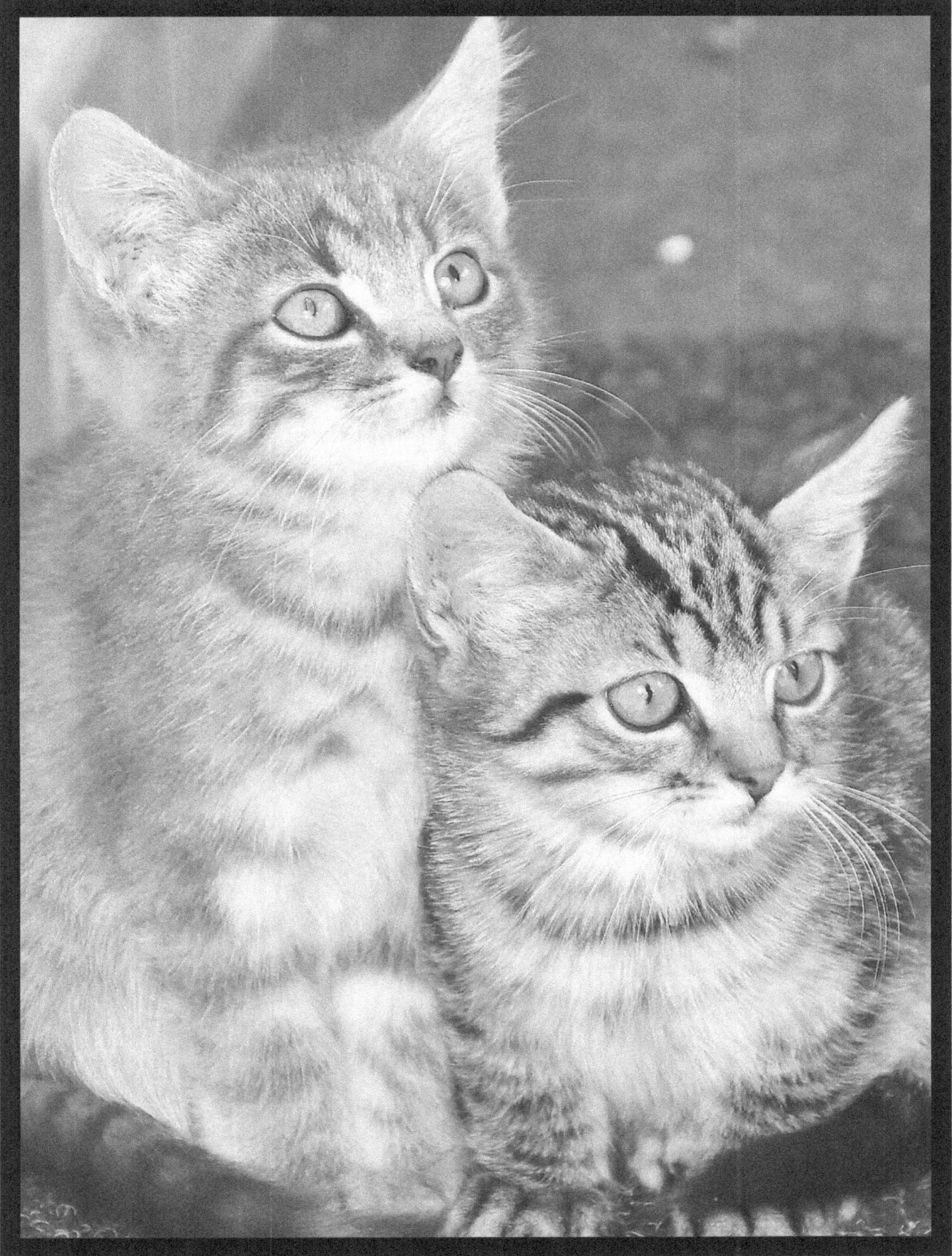

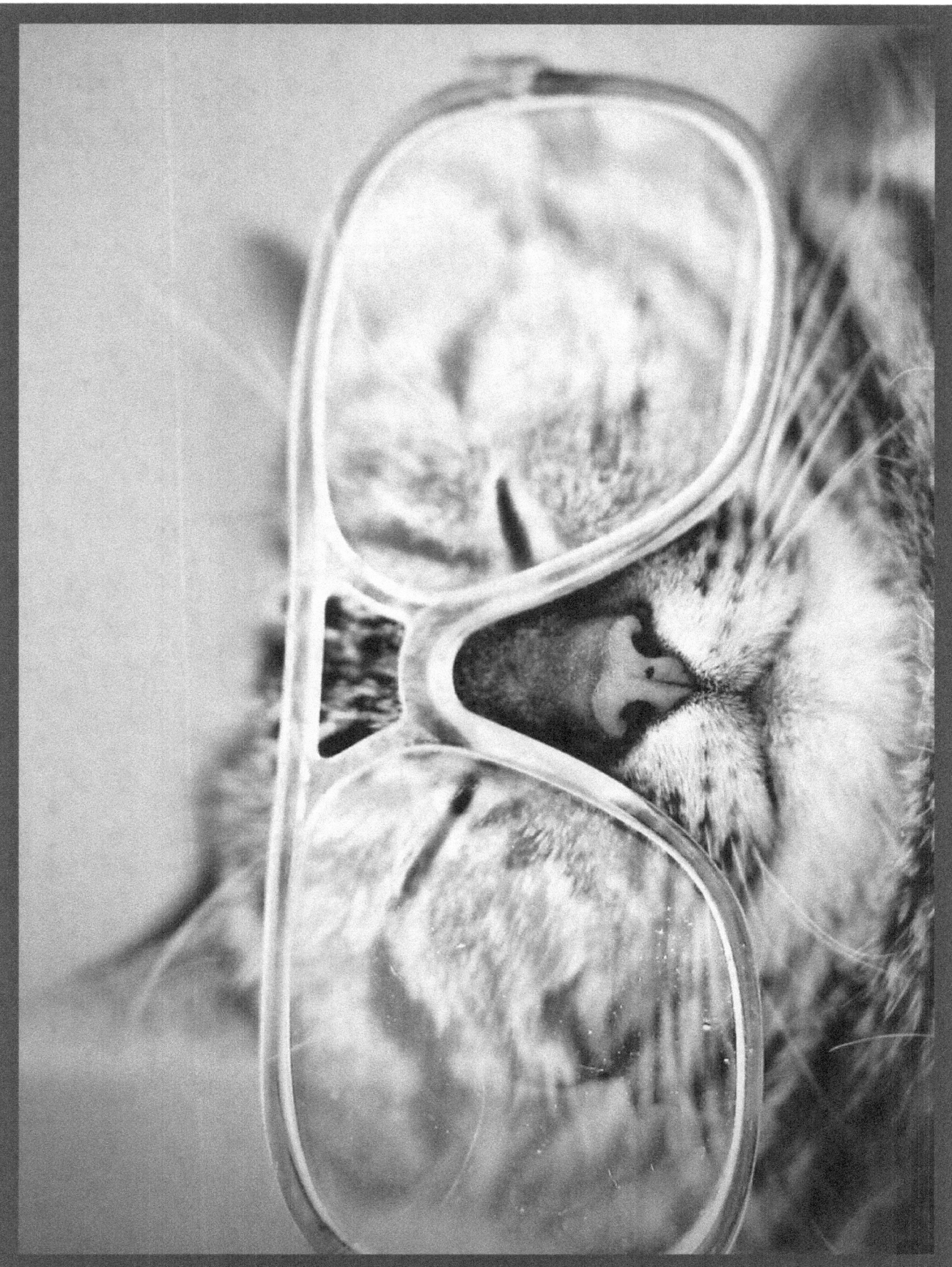

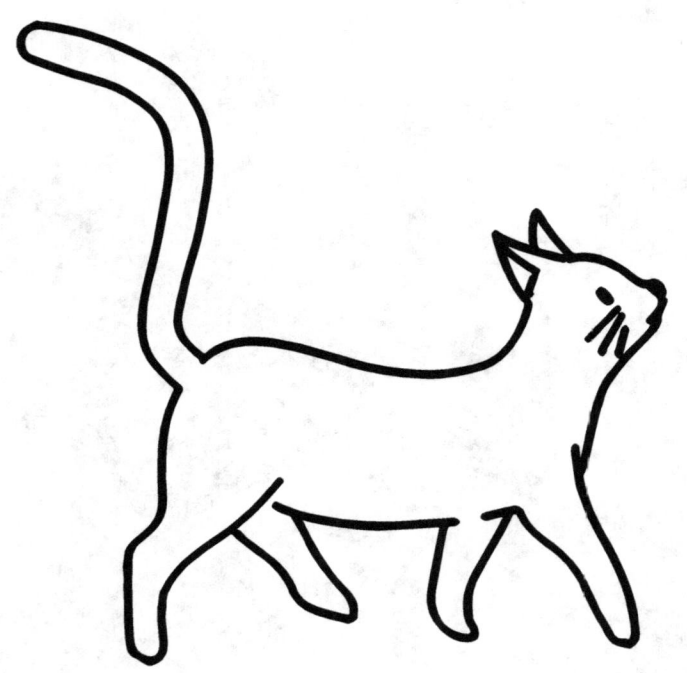

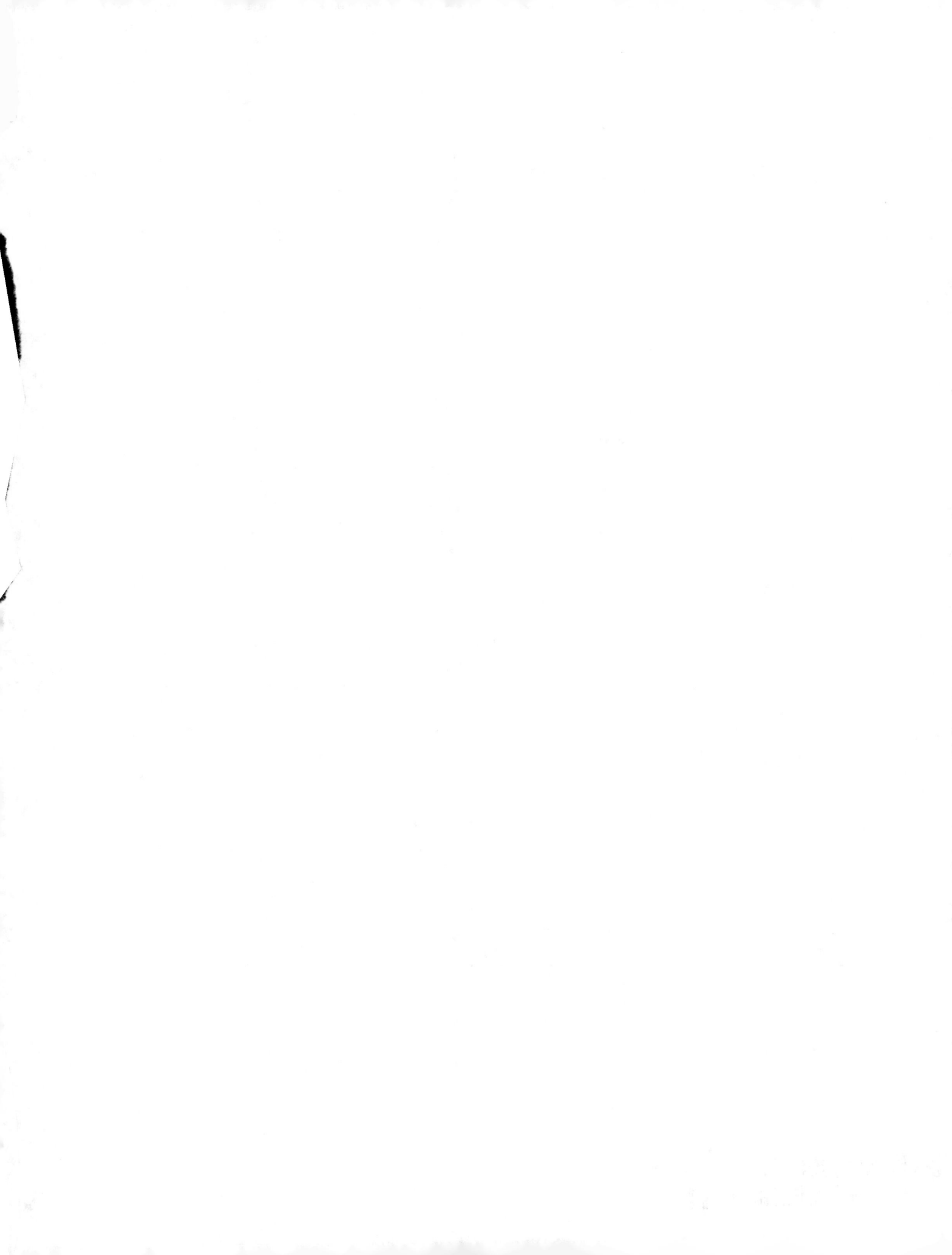